YOG

ITS PHILOSOPHY & PRACTICE

Easy and simple interpretation of the secrets of metaphysics for internal purification and meeting with our own soul through the eight yogic practices established by Saint Patanjali and practical yogic medication to cure diseases like diabetes, obesity, gas formation, constipation, piles, stomach problems, backache, cervical spondalitis, slip disc, wind problems, allergy, sinusitis, respiratory problem, migraine, depression, high blood pressure, stress, hyper cholestimia and heart diseases.

Swami Ramdev

Publisher	:	**DIVYA PRAKASHAN** **Divya Yog Mandir Trust** Kripalu Bagh Ashram, Kankhal Haridwar - 249408, Uttaranchal
E-mail	:	divyayoga@rediffmail.com
Website	:	www.divyayoga.com
Telephone	:	(01334) 244107, 240008, 246737
Fax	:	(01334) 244805

First Edition : 50,000 Copies, March 2005

Printer : **Sai Security Printers Limited**
152, DLF Industrial Area Faridabad (Haryana) 121003
Telephone: 95-129-2256819, 2257743, 2272277 Fax-95-129-2256239
E-mail: saipressindia@yahoo.com

Distributor : **Diamond Pocket Books (P). Ltd.**
X-30, Okhla Industrial Area, Phase-II, New Delhi-110020
Phone: 011-51611861, Fax: 011-51611866
E-mail:sales@diamondpublication.com
Website:www.diamondpublication.com

Price : **Rs. 125/-**

ISBN 81-89235-15-X

DEDICATION

ledicate this humble composition to the pious memory of Saint Brahmalin by rendering
y services to obtain the objective of health, spirituality and education of the Krupalu Bagh
hram, which was established by revered Saint Swami Shri Krupalu Dev Ji Maharaj in
32, who dedicated his entire life to the worship of God, spreading practice of yog and in
rvice of the nation. He was the harbinger of revolution and a great freedom fighter,
tirely devoted to the service of the nation, religion and culture. He managed and published
monthly magazine 'Vishwagyan' in enslaved India in order to free our motherland from
e clutches of the Britishers, and gave the message to the youth to dedicate their lives to
e nation. He united the brave martyrs and great freedom fighters like Ras Behari Bose,
e prime accused in the Lord Harding bomb case, who had taken shelter in the respected
vamiji's ashram.

- Swami Ramdev

PREFACE

It is heartening to present the English edition of this popular book, **Yog its Philosophy an**
Practice, written by the revered Swami Ramdevji Maharaj. The first edition of the Hin
book was published in the year 2002. In a span of just two years, this book has enable
thousands of devotees to be a part of yoga revolution . Superior quality of paper an
international style of printing has been used for this edition. Attractive photographs hav
added new dimension to this book. Despite increase in cost of research and productio
we tried our best to keep the price affordable for citizens so that book will continue t
enlighten generations to come.

Yog is complete in every aspect because it touches the every sphere of human life. It is
complete science which provides healthy lifestyle and a complete preventive medicatio
system and above all, an enlightening spiritual art..

The reason for popularity of Yog lies in the fact that it has never bound itself within th
narrow-minded attitude of sex, religion, caste, community, area and language. A devotee
philosopher, amateur, ascetic, unmarried, married or any person can get into the proximit
of yog and reap its benefits. It has proved to be beneficial not only in the uplifting of a
individual but also in the overall development of family, society, nation and the world. Th
answer of the problems like stress, unrest, terrorism, ignorance and incompleteness t
which the man of modern society is falling prey, lies only in Yog. It is a divine science, whic
brings the mankind on the path of positive thinking, which was discovered by the learne
saints and seers of ancient India. Saint Patanjali brought it in a disciplined manner, preserve
and produced the eight yogic practices in the form of Yog. Respected Swamiji advices an
practices these eight yogic practices in his discourses and yoga training camps. He ha
arrived at a conclusion that a healthy individual and a happy society can be built only unde
the shelter of Yog.

Yog is not only meant for the ascetics, devotees and yogis living in caves, but it is equall
important and beneficial for the ordinary people living with his/her family as well. It i
surprising to note that we are ready to fall into the trap of two hundred-year-old allopathi
system of medication and willingly victimising ourselves economically, physically and mentall
but are reluctant and ignorant towards thousands of years old yog knowledge, which is no
only practical but also a free medication system. Had this been just a mystic science, the
why would have Krishna given this advice to Arjun? Yograj Swami Ramdevji has done a grea

rvice by preserving this knowledge, which was loosing its base and re-establishing it for dian mankind. Therefore, he is not only worthy of respect and faith of millions of Indians t the entire world.

e are confident and zealous that with your co-operation, respect, faith and devotion, this volution of divine culture will continue to progress and take the ascending journey of cient spiritual knowledge including Yog and Ayurved from zero to infinity.

-**Acharya Balkrishna**
Divya Yog Mandir Trust,
Kankhal, Haridwar.

PERSONAL APPEAL

I bow every moment to the God present within us. He is the supreme power of the univers who bestows happiness to all mankind, with whose affection and compassion the who world is celebrating. HE is giving comfort, peace and prosperity to the creatures and givir shelter to a small person like me and filled my life with happiness.

With the grace of the supreme soul and pious deeds of my previous birth, I studied th entire literature, including Dayanand Saraswati's Veda, at the age of 14. As a result, n young heart got inspired to meet with the individual soul and study the original Vedas. It le my life onto the beneficial path of yog. As per God's will, I left home at the age of 15-16 an started the spiritual journey to discover knowledge of Veda, spirituality and pshyc philosophy. And, with God's grace, I got the proximity of saintly, learned, worshipper Brahma, Acharya Baldevaji Maharaj. He was kind enough to give me the knowledge Upanishads, Darshan, and Vedas, including the Sanskrit grammar of Paniniye. He bestowe upon me the real Brahmanism and made my life devoted towards Brahma.

I understand that, whatever is auspicious in my life it is because of the grace of precepto and whatever is inauspicious it is due to my ignorance. I cannot separate myself from th indebtedness of the ascetic, great soul, who is managing Gurukul and taking care of thousand of stray cattle and performing this religious sacrifice on the holy land of Haryana. After God I firstly offer my gratitude to the same preceptor.

After completing my education at Gurukul, respected Guruji offered me a post of religiou instructor at the Gurukul in his proximity but God wanted me to render my service elsewhere. After that, I took the responsibility of religious instructor at Gurukul Kisangarh Ghaseda under the proximity of the respected devotee and great soul Dharmavirji. But th Supreme Being had a different path for me. I came in contact of great, humble, learned an respected saint Acharya Karmavirji Maharaj while practicing Yog in the caves situated in th pious place, Gangotri with my gurukul mate, friend, devoted, helpful and learned Achary Balkrishanji. Gradually, God brought us all ascetics together. In the process of this union highly learned, holy, respected Acharya Shri Muktanandji and Acharya Shri Virendraji devote their services in the field of health, spirituality and education.

With the grace of revered and respected preceptor Swami Shri Shankardevji, this Divy Yog Mandir Trust was established in the year 1995 and became a medium of providin services to the entire nation. It has all been possible as a result of the devotion, sacrifice and meditation of the learned religious instructor mentioned above. I have written the present book as a simple being, Acharya has given me the inspiration, co-operation and consultation. Thanking all my friends wholeheartedly is purely self-applause.

I pray to the humble storekeeper of Bara Akhada, Kankhal, Shri Panchayati, respected Swami Shri Rajendra Dasji Maharaj, respected Mahamandelshwar Swami Hansdasji Maharaj and other sages of Haridwar who have always blessed the social, spiritual, cultural and educational services of the institution.

I pray to God to give healthy, happy, and long lives to Shri Dr. Yashdeva Shastriji, Shri Rambhartji, Dr. B.D.Sharmaji, Dr. V.Mukherjee who has always been willing to offer their selfless, devoted and humble services to the ashram and I also thank Pradip Kumar and others who have fulfilled their respective duties with complete devotion.

In the past several years, many huge yog devotion camps have been organized across the India, in which millions of people have participated and the demand of the Yog book has increased tremendously.

Due to the involvement in providing services, we were unable to publish the book in a systematic manner in spite of writing it seven years ago. But God was not willing to accept the inactivity of Divya Yog Mandir publishing work. For this purpose, resident of Rajasthan, devotee and helpful sage Shri Lakshmichandji Nagar, who had been associated with academics throughout his life and has worked in the capacity of Principal in Rajasthan Education Department, took the responsibility of proof reading, compilation and rearrangement of this divine publication .Solely due to his self- inspiration and tireless efforts this first edition is in your hands. I pray to God to bestow upon him a healthy, long life full of spiritualism, through which he can render maximum services.

I offer my sincere thanks to all those gentlemen who have contributed directly or indirectly in the writing or other works of the book. I specially thank respected Swami Shri Aparekshanandji Maharaj for his special task.

The co-operation of trustee of Divya Yog Mandir Trust, Shri Upendra Bhai and Shri Babu Bhai Patel, Ahmedabad, Shri Jivraj Bhai Patel, Surat and Ramnivasji Garg, Delhi has been of great help in the publication of this book. I pray God to bestow honesty, strength, devotion, health, longevity, material and spiritualistic prosperity to all the devoted persons who have always offered their complete services to the tasks managed by the ashram, through which the social work has gathered momentum.

I thank Sai Security Printers for bringing out the English Edition of this book in a grand manner.

There may be a possibility of mistakes in the book due to involvement in social work. The feedback received from the learned readers with respect to the mistakes will be taken care of in the next edition. *Om sham!*

- Swami Ramdev

Contents

Contents

Introduction to Yog

Form of Yog :

The word 'Yog' has been used in Vedas, Upanishads, Gita and mythological scriptures etc. since ancient times. It is a very important terminology in Indian 'Darshan'. From devotion to self-emancipation to the work arena, it has been widely used in our classics. According to Saint Patanjali, spiritual instructor of Yog Darshan, "Yog is the ability to develop restrain on earthly desires. Yog is a method through which a man overcomes these five tendencies of facts, transposition, alternative, sleep and memory; through practice and detachment. His soul become merely observatory and then he attains the stage of super consciousness.

According to Saint Vyas, "Yog is deep meditation". According to classical grammar, the word 'Yog' is derived from the deep knowledge of connecting humors of the body. It has been described in *Dhatupath* by sage Panini in the chapter *Divadigan* as connecting with deep meditation, in *Rudhiradigan* as connecting with Yog, and in *Churadigan* as connecting with patience, in these meanings the word connecting humors is used. In short, we can say that devoting ourselves with patience and connecting the individual soul with the supreme soul and attaining the bliss of deep meditation is Yog.

According to the conceptions of the above mentioned sages, Yog means combining self consciousness with the supreme soul who is the generator of the consciousness. If a person rises above all temporary desires and emotions and is engulfed with the emotion of detachment then he comes in contact with the supreme consciousness.

There are five stages of the consciousness— clarity, stupidity, confusion, concentration and highest contemplation. In the first three conditions, Yog or deep meditation does not take place. In the conditions of concentration, when the five obstacles i.e., ignorance, attachment, hatred, affection cease to exist due to ignorance, and the bonds of karma becomes weak then contemplation accompanied by reasoning, thinking, happiness and pride takes place. In this case, highest contemplation takes place, which is not associated with any idol, thing or meaning.

In the Indian mythology, Gita has a special place. The modern Indian sages have propagated Gita all over the world. The Lord of Yog, Shri Krishna has been referred in Gita with various meanings.

To be contented and remain stable in favorable-unfavorable conditions, success-failure, accomplishment-non-accomplishment, victory-loss is called Yog. To get inspired by internal inspiration and look into the soul with clear mind and work skillfully has been considered Yog in Gita.

According to Jain religious instructors, Yog is the resource with which the soul is accomplished and salvation is achieved. In other references of *Jain Darshan*, KarmaYog is the condition of mind, speech and body.

According to the modern-age sage Shri Arvind, the efforts made to attain solemnity with God and attaining it is the form of Yog.

Types of Yog

There are four types of Yog viz. Mantra Yog, Yog of Concentration, Austerity and Kingship have been described in Yog classic of *Dattatreya* and *Yograj Upanishad*. The symptoms of these four types of Yog have been described in the elementary Upanishad of Yog.

1. Yog of mantras - The devotee attains unsightly accomplishment by chanting the mantras of matrikas (Goddess of Tantrika - Brahma, Maheshwari, Koumari, Vaishnavi, Varahi, Indrani and Chamunda) systematically and continuously for 12 years,

2. Yog of Concentration - Thinking of God along with the daily activities is called Yog of concentration.

3. Austerity (HathYog) - Practicing various *asanas, mudras, pranayam* and difficult postures and making the body pure and concentration of the mind is called austerity.

4. Combination of planets in a person's nativity leading to kingship- Resisting the passions and practicing Yam -Niyam to make the soul pure and let it meet with the internal soul by enlightening the soul is called kingship. The meaning of the word RajYog is '*Rajru deeptou*', to enlighten the kingdom and meaning of enlightenment and Yog is experience of deep meditation.

Gita contains detailed analysis of Yog with meditation, Yog with karmas and naturalism (SankhyaYog).

The 15th chapter of Gita considers Yog of asceticism and karma as the Yog of highest order.

Saint Patanjali has described the maxims of Yog by aiming at the eight yogic practices. When we look into the classics of Yog to know the secrets, we arrive at a conclusion that whatever methods and processes were popular for attaining spiritual devotion, they all have been spoken of in the name of Yog.

---

1. योगश्चित्तवृत्ति निरोधः Yog Darshan 1/2
2. प्रमाणविपर्यय विकल्प निद्रा स्मृतयः Yog Darshan 1/6
3. अभ्यास वैराग्याभ्यां तन्निरोधः Yog Darshan 1/12
4. तदा द्रष्टुः स्वरूपेऽवस्थानम् 1/3
5. योगः समाधिः व्यास भाष्य Yog Darshan 1/1
6. ज्ञानस्यैव पराकाष्ठा वैराग्यम्। Vyasbhashyam Yog Darshan 1/16
7. क्षिप्तं मूढं विक्षिप्तमेकाग्रं निरुद्धमिति चित्तभूमयः। Vyasbhashyam Yog Darshan 1/1
8. योगस्थ कुरू कर्माणि सङ्ग त्यक्त्वा धनंजय।
   सिद्धयसिद्धयो समाभूत्वा समत्वं योग उच्यते। Gita 2/48
9. योगः कर्मसु कौशलम्। Gita 1/50
10. मोक्षेण योजनादेव योगो ह्यत्र निरुच्यते (यशोविजय कृत द्वात्रिंशिका १०/१ (मुक्खेण जोयणाओ जोगो हरिभद्र सूरिकृता योग विशंका १)
11. कायवाड्मनः कर्मयोगः Tatwaarthasutra 6/1
12. श्री अरिवन्द Yog Samanvaya pg 605
13. मन्त्रयोगो लयश्चैव हठयोगस्तथैव च। राजयोगश्चतुर्थः स्यादयोगानामुत्तमस्तु स। Datta Yog 18,19
14. योग तत्वोपनिषद् श्लोक 21 to 25
15. ध्यानोनात्मनि पश्यन्ति केचिदात्मानमात्मना। अन्ये सांख्येन योगेन कर्मयोगेन चापरे। Gita 3/24
16. संन्यासः कमैयोगश्च निःश्रेयस्कारावुभौ।
    तयोस्तु कर्मसंन्यासात् कर्मयोगो विशिष्यते। Gita 5/2

Effect of Yog on the body

Yog allows us to know our self. It strengthens our inner power to meet the supreme soul and attain complete bliss. Indian sages have defined different types of Yog. Here, we will be discussing about the asanas (postures) and pranayam yogs in detail which come under the eight yogic practices (resistance towards passions, rules, postures i.e., asana, controlling the breath i.e. pranayam, resisting the sense organs, concentration, meditation and deep meditation), six other yogic exercises of austerity (Hathyog) will also be discussed. Practicing yog revives our dead consciousness. These exercises rejuvenate dead tissues and thus new tissues and cells are formed. Light yogic exercises reactivate the nervous system, and regulate blood circulation. It reinstates fresh energy in the body. According to the laws of physical science, when the body contracts and expands, energy is developed and diseases get cured. This activity is done simply with the help of different yogic asanas. With the practice of pranayam and other asanas, the glands and muscles of the body repel-attract, contract-expand, which cures diseases naturally.

Yog also keeps the veins healthy. Pancreas becomes active and produces insulin in the right quantity, which helps in curing diabetes and other diseases. Health is directly linked with the digestive system. A bad digestive system is the prime reason for most of the diseases. Even some serious problems like heart disease occur due to a bad digestive system. Yog strengthens the entire digestion process, making every part of the body healthy, light and active. Fresh air enters the lungs, which keep diseases like asthma, respiratory problems, allergy etc. away. Fresh air also strengthens the heart. Yogic exercises dissolve the fat, which makes the body light and it remains healthy, fit and attractive. Not only that, Yog is beneficial for thin and lean bodies as well. Yog controls the mind and senses, it helps the follower to get out of the darkness. तदा द टु स्वरूपेअवस्थानम् In this way we can embark on the path of Yog and experience the inner happiness of meeting the supreme being and attain physical & mental, intelligence and spiritual progress.

Daily routine of a healthy person

Good health is the key to all the happiness. An unhealthy body is like a graveyard. Who is healthy? Sage writes in the Ayurveda text *Sushrut*:

समदोषाः समाग्निश्च समधातुमलक्रियः ।
प्रसन्नात्मेन्द्रियमनः स्वस्थइत्यभिधीयते ।।

(sushruth sutra - 15/41)

This means, a person who has all the three humors- wind, bile and phlegm in equal quantity, the fire of the stomach is normal (neither very less nor very high), Body contains the seven substances - essence, blood, flesh, fat, bones, marrow and sperm are in the required quantity, urination and excretion is normal, the ten senses (ears, nose, eyes, skin, taste, rectum, genital organs, hands, legs and tongue), mind and their ruler i.e., the soul remain happy then such a person is said to be healthy. The sages have given a broad and scientific definition to the word health. The three pillars to attain this healthiness are diet, sleep and celibacy.

त्रयोपस्तभा आहारनिद्राब्रह्मचर्यमिति (*Charak Sutra 11/34*) -these are the three pillars on which the whole body rests. God of Yog Shri Krishna says in *Gita*:

युक्ताहारविहारस्य युक्तचेष्टस्य कर्मसु।
युक्तस्वप्नावबोधस्य योगो भवति दुःखहा॥   (*Gita - 6/17*)

The person whose diet, sexual happiness, thoughts and behaviour are under control and whose deeds have divinity, there is always piousness in the mind and desire towards auspicious things, whose sleep and awakening is meaningful, he is the true yogi. We will discuss about the three pillars and other rules in brief.

1. Diet :

यथाखाद्यतेऽन्नं तथा सम्पद्यतेमनः
यथा पीयते वारि तथा निगद्यते वचः।

It means a person's body develops with diet. Diet has its effect not only on the body but also on the mind.

आहारशुद्धौ सत्वशुद्धिः सत्वशुद्धौ ध्रुवा स्मृतिः।
स्मृतिलब्धे सर्वग्रन्थीनां विप्रमोक्षः॥

(*Chandogyopanishad*)

Saint Charak has given an interesting anecdote with reference to diet. Once Saint Charak asked his disciples, "Who is not patient? in other words, who is healthy? His best disciple Vagbhatt replied, "A person who does good deeds, eats as much as required and in accordance with the season, is healthy". One should eat according to one's constitution (wind, bile and phlegm). If the constitution is windy and wind related problems arise in the body then rice, wind-affected and sour foods should be avoided. Pepper, dry ginger powder and ginger should always be consumed. If the constitution is bile then hot, spicy and fried food items should not be consumed. Raw foods like gourd, cucumber etc. are beneficial. People with phlegm constitution should not eat cold stuffs like rice, curd, buttermilk etc. in excess quantity. Pepper and turmeric should be added to milk and then consumed. Food should be taken in the right quantity. Half portion of the stomach should be reserved for grains, one-fourth for liquid items and remaining should be left for wind. If the food items are consumed in accordance to the season then diseases do not attack the person. There should be a fixed time for having meals. Food consumed at irregular intervals causes indigestion and other diseases. Fruits and some light liquid items should be taken in the morning between 8 and 9 am. Lesser the quantity of grains taken in the morning, the better it is for the body. Persons who are above 50 years of age should not consume stale food. Meals should be taken between 11 and 12 in the afternoon. Taking meals between 12 and 1 in the afternoon is considered to be medium and after that it is considered to be bad. In the evening, the period between 7 to 8 P.M is considered to be the best, between 8 and 9 is medium and after that it is bad. One should not talk while eating as the food is not properly chewed and gets consumed in excess. Therefore, one should be silent while eating and should chew the food properly. One morsel should be chewed 32 times or at least 20 times. Chewing habit reduces the violent tendency, because we all are aware of the fact that when a person gets angry he bites his teeth, which means tooth is the origin of anger. If we want to eliminate the violent tendencies, we should pay special attention to chewing the food. You will know the results only after having its first hand experience. One should begin to eat the food by chanting 'Om' or the 'Gayatri Mantra' and sip the water at least three times. One should not drink water while eating food. If the food is dry then water can be taken in little quantity. Do not drink more than two to three sips of water after eating food. If buttermilk is available then it should be taken. There is a verse in Sanskrit which says, "A person who drinks water in the morning after waking up, drinks milk after dinner and buttermilk after lunch, he never needs a doctor". In other words, that person remains healthy. Along with that our food should be completely perfect. The meal should include minerals, salts and vitamin-B. The food should not include eggs, meat etc. God has made us vegetarian. When we can live on chapatis, which does not involve any violence, then what is the need to kill any creature? It is better to die than living such a life. Human qualities like pity, sympathy, compassion, love, respect etc. get destroyed by eating non-vegetarian food and the stomach becomes like a graveyard.

2. Sleep :

Sleep is an internal experience in itself. If a person does not get proper sleep, then he can even become lunatic. One cannot understand the meaning of sleep, but one who does not get proper sleep can understand its importance. A healthy person requires six hours of sleep. Children and elderly people require eight hours of sleep. The life of a person who goes to bed early and wakes up early is of high quality.

God has created the nature in such a manner that the human beings, birds, animals and other creatures get back to their dwellings after the sunset. All the birds, except owl and bat wake up early in the morning and start their work with the name of God. The cock gives the message to wake up at dawn. The birds are seen chirping the God's name, but the unlucky human being remains awake the whole night like an owl and lies on the bed without enjoying the dawn and becomes sick in the end. We can also get the inspiration from these dumb creatures. Sleeping and waking up early makes a person healthy and pleased.

3. Celibacy :

Diverting our minds from materialistic subjects and concentrating on spiritualism and social work is called celibacy. Celibacy is not just controlling the senses of

God's name, but the unlucky human being remains awake the whole night like an owl and lies on the bed without enjoying the dawn and becomes sick in the end. We can also get the inspiration from these dumb creatures. Sleeping and waking up early makes a person healthy and pleased.

3. Celibacy : Diverting our minds from materialistic subjects and concentrating on spiritualism and social works is called celibacy. Celibacy is not just controlling the senses of genital organs. Transforming the strengths of senses and mind and turning them towards the soul and attaining Brahma is celibacy.

भोगो न भुक्ता वयमेव भुक्तास्तपो न तसं वयमेव तसा ।
कालो न यातो वयमेव याता तृष्णा न जीर्णा वयमेव जीर्णा॥

(Bharturishatkavairagya - 12)

This means, we do not experience the pleasure or pain, but things experience us. Devotion does not devote, we devote ourselves, time does not end, we merge into time. Desires do not destroy, we get destroyed. We never get the satisfaction after attaining something, instead the desires become more and more strong in turn. Saint Manu says:

न जातु काम कामानामुभोगेन शाम्यति
हविषाकृष्णवत्मैंव भूय एवाभिवर्द्धते ॥

(Manusmruti 2)

Sex does not calm down by experiencing it, rather the lust becomes more vigorous after having experienced it. In the same way, desires increase more and more when we experience the things. Saint Kapil says in Sankhya Darshan:

न भोगात् रागशान्तिर्मुनिवत्

(Sankhya Darshan 4/27)

This means, nature is advising us to follow the limits. Let us be a part of this respected nature.

4. Exercise : Just as our body needs diet for a proper functioning, in the same way asana, pranayam and other exercises are extremely necessary for it. In the lack of exercise, body looses its charm and attraction, and becomes unhealthy. Whereas, regular exercises transforms a weak, ugly and diseased person into healthy, strong and beautiful one. The main reasons for heart disease, diabetes, wind related problems, piles, gas, blood pressure, mental stress etc. is lack of exercise. If Yoga is practiced

regularly then these diseases will never occur. Amongst the various yogic exercises, asana and pranayam are the best.

Although other exercises do involve physical work outs but the concentration of the mind and peace is not achieved through it. Heavy exercises do benefit muscles, but not the nervous system. Gradually, the muscles become so heavy that the blood circulation in stops and it starts paining. Whereas asana and pranayam provide a wholesome benefit, be it mental or physical aspect of the one's body.

5. Bath :
After asana, when the body temperature becomes normal, one should take bath. Bath refreshes the body, unnecessary heat gets washed out and the body becomes light and fresh.

अद्भिर्गत्राणि शुध्यन्ति मन सत्येन शुध्यति।
विद्यातपो यां भूतात्मा बुद्धिर्ज्ञानिन शुध्यति॥

(Manusmriti) 5/1

Water purifies the body. Truth purifies the mind. Knowledge and devotion purifies both the brain and the soul. Except sick persons, one should take bath with cold water. Taking bath with hot water weakens the eyesight and digestive system. Hair starts graying and falling prematurely. Unnecessary heat is caused in the body and humors get destroyed. One should pat the body with a khadi towel after taking bath. This increases the shine. If the person has constipation then the stomach should be rubbed with the towel. However, swimming and taking bath in a river or a pond is considered the best.

6. Meditation :
A person aspiring for peace, happiness and comforts should pray and worship the God at least for 15 minutes and up to one hour after completing the daily chores like purification, bath and exercises. The meditation done for a long time with devotion by chanting the Gayatri mantra and Pranav (omkar) gives lot of strength, peace and happiness.

Eight Yogic Practices (Ashtang Yoga)

Utility of eight yogic practices :

Everybody in this world desires peace and happiness and whatever a person is doing in this world is with an objective, he thinks that he will attain happiness with that. Not only the individuals, but all the nations of the world are of the opinion that peace should prevail in the world. Every year, a person who devotes himself to establish peace whole-heartedly is awarded a noble prize for peace. However, all are confused as to how this peace can be established. All have their own perspective but none has come to any common conclusion as yet. One person says that until only Islam or Christianity will not prevail, peace cannot be attained. The other person says that if everybody comes under the shelter of Buddha or Mahavira then peace and happiness will be everywhere.

There are a number of communities, beliefs and preachers and preceptors in India, and everybody claims that if one follows the path as directed by them, only then peace and happiness can be achieved. However, all these preachers, communities and so called Islamists, Budhism and Jainism do not have that generosity, broadness, completeness, which can be accepted by the entire mankind. They all have their own limitations.

Murderous wars have taken place in the world to establish legacy of so called religions and castes but no results was obtained. Violence is increasing day by day. This means that the solutions which the people are planning to implement have the capacity but lack completeness, perfection and broadness. On the one hand, a person derives happiness for some time by accepting these sectarians, communities and so called religions, and on the other hand, he gets into the trap of superstitions, evil practices and myths that it has become difficult for him to come out of their clutches. He is also deprived of complete truth. Not only that even if a person accepts the so called Islam and Islamism, a question mark is seen on the nation's integrity and unity. The nation starts loosing its power. In such a situation, the religion itself is dangerous for the nation. But can't something crop up that can be followed by every individual of this world? Can't there be some rules, limitations and faiths, which can be followed by all? Which won't disintegrate the people a nation and neither it serves the selfish interests of individuals, which can be acceptable to all and can help in attaining complete satisfaction, peace and comforts. This is the eight yogic practices instructed by Saint Patanjali. This is not a belief or community but a method of leading your life. If the people of the world are serious about establishing peace then the only solution lies in the following eight yogic principles. A person can experience the individual and social

Yog Sadhna
&
Yoga Healing Secrets

equality, physical health, intellectual awareness, mental peace and happiness of the soul by following eight yogic principles. Now we shall talk about the eight yogic exercises in brief. Saint Patanjali writes in Yoga maxims:

यमनियमासनप्राणायामप्रत्याहारधायणाध्यानसमाध्य अष्टौ अड्गनि॥

(Yoga Darshan 2/29)

Rresistance to passions, rules, asana, pranayam, senses, meditation, and deep meditation are the eight principles of Yoga.

A person cannot become a yogi without following these principles. These eight principles are not only for a yogi but whoever wishes to be completely happy in his life and wants all the living beings to be happy. These eight yogic principles aptly prove themselves towards every challenge of religion, spiritualism, humanity and science. If anything can stop these murderous wars, it is only these eight yogic principles. Eight yogic principles include behaviour in a normal life to highest level of spiritual condition along with meditation and deep meditation. Any person who is exploring his existence and wants to introduce himself with the ultimate truth of life, he should follow the eight yogic principles. Resistance to passions and rules are the basis of Ahstang yoga (eight yogic principles).

Resistance towards passions : the first principle of Ashtang Yoga is resistance towards passions (Yama). The word 'yama' completes with the word 'yama uparame' humor, which means, यम्यन्ते उपरम्यन्ते निवर्त्यन्ते हिंसादिम्य इन्द्रियाणि यैस्तै यमा। it means following this deviates the senses and the mind from violence and other inauspicious feelings and concentrates on the soul, these are resistance towards passions. Saint Patanjali has described these yamas as follow-

अहिंसासत्यास्तेयब्रह्मचर्यापरिग्रहा यमा।।

(Yoga Darshan 2/30)

Non- violence, truth, not stealing others' things, celibacy and not collecting unwanted things - are the five yamas. We now describe each one of them in brief.

1. Non-Violence : non-violence means not troubling a person through mind, speech or deeds. Not to wish bad for anybody, not to hurt a person through bad words, and not to kill a creature in any condition, at any place, any day, this is non-violence. Saint Vyas also says that:

तत्राहिंसा सर्वथा सर्वदा सर्वभूतानामनभिद्रोह

(Vyasbhashya, YogaDarshan)

2. Truth : Truth is to have the pure feeling in mind based on what you have seen, heard and known, the same thing should be adopted in the speech and actions should be done according to that. One should not speak such words to others, which are deceiving, confusing and which has no meaning. One should speak such words which do not hurt other creatures. Speech should be beneficial for everybody. The speech which harms others is sinful and therefore causes grief. Therefore, one should test and use the speech which is beneficial for all the living creatures. Saint Vyas says the same thing with respect to truth "सत्यं यथार्थे वाङ्मनसि। यथादृष्टं यथानुमितं यथाश्रुतं तथा वाङ्मनश्चेति। परत्र स्वाबोधक्रान्ते वागयुक्ता सा यदि न वाचिता भ्रान्ता वा प्रतिपत्तिवन्ध्या वा भवदिति। एषा सर्वाभूतोपकारार्थं प्रवत्ता न भूतोपघाताय।"

(Vyabhashya, YogaDarshan)

3. Not Stealing others things:
Taking hold of others things without their permission, and acquiring the things against the directives of the classical texts is called stealing. A desire to acquire others' things is also stealing. Therefore a yogi should never steal, rather he should feel contented with whatever the God has given and should be happy in that much only.

4. Celibacy :
Sacrificing the food items which arise sexual desires, sacrificing scenes, hearing and dressing up and to be a celibate by protecting the chastity is called celibacy. Eight types of sexual intercourse - looking at somebody with lust, touching somebody, meeting alone, talking, discussing the subject, mutual enactment, thought of sex and company are the eight types of intercourse. A celibate should protect himself from all these things and always control his senses and inspire his senses - eyes, ears, nose, skin, and taste towards auspicious things and always think of descent, good things and missions of his life. A devotee should always keep in his mind that his natural condition is free of defects. As the natural quality of water is coolness and flowing. Freezing, becoming hot, vaporizing and evaporation are not the natural qualities and even after getting heated, evaporating and converting into snow and becoming solid and then coming back to its original form. In the same way celibacy is our natural form. To sit and meditate in a quiet place and to introspect and see whether there is lust inside or not. Do you have lust, anger, greed, attachment, and ego and other faults? Then you will find that you do not have these faults. These faults are created through invitation. These faults enter our bodies like thieves, stay for a while and within that time steal the strength of our body, mind and soul, deform it and destroys and vanishes everything. Lust and anger attack for sometime and during that period these faults tremor the whole body, make the body charmless, strengthless and shineless, they dissolve toxic substances in the body. We are stolen again and again and keep on saying that it is natural to be stolen, we cannot protect ourselves. Then my dear friend nobody can protect you. Wake up, rise and recognize your natural duty. Faults are not your real duties, these are exterior duties and Lord Shri Krishna says in Gita: स्वधर्मे निधनं श्रेय परधर्मो भयावह। Do not burn yourself in the kiln of lust, anger, greed, attachment and ego. You are the soul, your natural qualities are friendship, sympathy, love, empathy, service, devotion, helping others, happiness and peace. You are faultless,

we invite the faults, call them, just like a person first collects things of wealth and richness and then invites the thieves and when the thieves conquer the house, land and building, steal everything and we stand and watch when we are stolen and say, "Oh! What has happened! I have just called them and now they are robbing everything! Destroying everything!" But a person never invites the thieves to steal the external property because he has himself collected the luxury and richness, he cannot see them being robbed. But, oh man just think, there is an unlimited happiness, peace, lot of comfort, strength, charm, sharpness, power, intelligence, courage, friendship, sympathy, compassion and other unending luxury within you, which the God has given you. So, why do you destroy them by inviting thieves like anger, lust and other faults and then you say that it is natural, what should I do? At least now control yourself, recognize the strength given by God. Establish the strong determination within yourself that you are faultless, celibacy is my prime duty, it is natural to remain celibate and treat it to be definite that after the unnatural and short termed flow and outburst of these faults, you have to lead a life in a faultless situation. Therefore do not throw yourself in the fire of faults. Be accomplished with the divine strengths given by God and follow celibacy and obtain peace and unlimited happiness, feel the broad and wide happiness from within. Follow celibacy and become sharp, clever, intelligent, strong and courageous and have divine love towards others, serve the people, make yourself beautiful by helping others and having sympathy. Walk on the path of Yoga devotion, only then you can recognise the happy form of God present within you. This is the ultimate truth. This is the objective of life.

5. Not collecting the unwanted things : Collection means, to try to collect the things from all sides. To lead a life which is just the reverse, one should be satisfied with minimum wealth, clothes, items and houses and to keep the main objective of devotion towards God is not collection. Whatever wealth, luxury and building and other richness is available according to God's arrangement, they should not be considered own by coming into the grip of ego. The devotee should not aspire for physical and external sources of happiness. Lead a life without any interest and make others happy with whatever things of joy and comforts are available. Saint Vyas says,

विषयाणामर्जनरक्षणक्षयसंगहिंसादोषदर्शनादस्वीकरणमपरिग्रह

(Vyasbhashya, yogadarshan)

Fault in the collection of the things of pleasure in the form of wealth, matter etc, protection- meaning fault in the protection of collected things, deterioration - fault in the deterioration of the collected things, attachments - fault in getting attracted towards the collected things and violence - नानुपहत्य भूतान्युपभोग संभवति meaning: it is not possible to obtain happiness without hurting other creatures. Therefore the material happiness involves the fault of violence. Therefore a yogi should maintain distance from materialism and not collect the unwanted things. In all these resistance towards passions, following non-violence and truth through mind, speech and actions and one should not have any sorts of limits in this. Saint Patanjali says,

जातिदेशकालसमयानवच्छिन्ना सार्वभौमा महाव्रत

(Yogadarshan 2/31)

In other words, complete and unbounded by the limits of nation, caste, time and period and whole-heartedly following non-violence in every situation is called the great ritual of non-violence. From an ordinary person's point of view, lot of difficulties arise in following these rituals. Therefore a person fixes some limits and bounds to these non-violence, not collecting things and truth to himself with respect to caste, country, time, period etc. For example, let us take non-violence, a person is a fisherman, he kills fish and sells and eats. This is his violence, but he does not kill cow, sheep and goats, this is his healing non-violence. But this will not be non-violence which is full of non-violence because this non-violence is bounded in the caste. In the same way non-violence is bounded in the borders of nations: For instance, I will not involve into violence in Kashi, Mathura and Haridwar and other holy places, that means I can indulge into violence in other places except the holy places. A person with such thinking is non-violent only till the limits of a place, he is not completely non-violent. The same thing applies to time, for instance, I will not indulge into non-violence on Ekadashi, full moon, new moon and Tuesdays etc. or on any festival. This is the non-violence bounded in time frame. The same is related to time limits, I will not do violence in normal situations but during special instances when I face some trouble I will do violence. This is also not complete non-violence. Complete non-violence will take place when everybody rises above limits and follow them every time, everywhere and at all the places, towards all creatures, in all situations, and in all circumstances without any deception in a simple way. The same should be understood with respect to truth, not stealing others things and not collecting unwanted things. For example normally I will tell lies to protect a brahman or a cow. This is caste based non-violenvce. I will speak truth in my country, place, in other words Haridwar and other holy places, Gurukul, mutt, temple, Gurudwara, Mosque, and Church etc. In other places of business, court and other official works I will speak lies. In the same time bound non-violence- I will not speak lies on special occasions like Ekadashi, and other time bound occasions and not in normal course, these are all not complete truth. Likewise not stealing others things, celibacy and not collecting unwanted things should also be understood. A devotee should rise above all these limitations of mind, speech and actions and follow the principles of resistance towards passions.

Rules :

The second basic factor in Yoga principles is rules. Saint Patanjali says:

शौचसन्तोषतप स्वाध्यायेश्वयप्रणिधानानि नियमा।

(Yogadarshan. 2/32)

This means excretion, satisfaction, devotion, regular study of Vedas and deep devotion towards God are the five rules.

1. Excretion :
Excretion is purification, cleanliness. Excretion or purification is of two types - one is external and the second is internal. Saint Manu has said aptly with respect to excretion.

अद्भिर्गात्राणि शुध्यन्ति मन सत्येन शुध्यति ।
विद्यातपो यां भूतात्मा बुद्धिर्ज्ञानेन शुध्यति।।

(Manusmriti 5-9)

It means the devotee should purify his body with water everyday, purify his mind with good behaviour, purify his soul with the study of Vedas and devotion and purify his intelligence with knowledge. The holy water of the Ganga can also purify the body. One has to follow the advises of the saints and sages for the purification of mind, brain and soul.

2. Satisfaction :
one should fulfill ones objective with the available resources. To be fully satisfied with whatever results are obtained and not to desire for the things which have not been achieved and whatever is achieved with the grace of God, not to discard it and not to aspire for the unavailable things is satisfaction. Saint Vyas says -

संतोषामृतततप्सानां यत्सुखं शान्तचेतसाम् ।
कु तस्तद्धनलुब्धानामितश्चेनश्च धावताम् ।।

This means consuming the nectar in the form of satisfaction gives immense internal happiness to the calm hearted people, that can never be achieved by people who are wandering here and there in the search of wealth and luxury. It has been said elsewhere that, संतोषमूलं हि सुखं दुखमूलं विपर्ययं The main factor for happiness is satisfaction and in the opposite case the basis for unhappiness is desire and aspirations. Sage says in Upanishads, ''न वित्तेन तर्पणीयो मनुष्य ...'' that means a man never gets satisfaction with wealth. Therefore the devotee should fulfill his duty and whatever results God gives according to his justice and arrangement, one should feel fully contended and never forget that the God blesses us with more beauty, youth, wealth, prosperity and entire luxury more than what we are worthy of.

3. Devotion :
Saint Vyas says that devotion means tolerating the challenges. He says, ''तपो द्वन्द्व सहनम्'' .This means whatever pains, troubles, adversities come in the path of accomplishment of objectives, they should be accepted easily, and marched forward towards our goal continuously and without deviating ourselves. In Mahabharta, Yaksh asks Yudhishtara, 'तपस किंम लक्षणमम्' "What is the quality of devotion?". King Yudhishtara replies, 'तप स्वदार्म वर्तित्वम्' Oh, Yaksha, whatever hardships, obstacles come in the path of duty, tolerating them and continuously devoting yourself to fulfill your duties is devotion. These hardships are-hunger-thirst, cold-hot, happiness- unhappiness, gain-

loss, fame-dishonour, worship-insult, honour-dishonour, victory-loss etc. To remain same in all these adversities is devotion, it is not just standing in fire or standing on one foot and giving pain to your body.

4. Regualr study of the Vedas :
Saint Vyas says, "प्रणवादि पवित्राणां जपो मोक्षशास्त्राणामध्ययनं वा this means that chanting omkar (pranav) mantra, true classics, Gita, Yoga darshan, Veda-Upanishad with devotion is called regular study of Vedas. If we look at the verbal meaning of regular study of Vedas, we derive two meanings. One is, which is the best study, the study of the good classics instructed by the sages is regular study of Vedas. We get purity by developing good thoughts and deeds, divinity and determination and purity of thoughts and determination makes our lives pious. The meaning of second study is studying ourselves, or studying our internal self, thinking about our existence, thoughts and introspect that who am I? What should I do? What am I doing? What is the aim of my life? Who gave me birth? Why have I born?

In this way the devotee should be alert and think with wisdom, then he will not come into the clutches of luxury and perform devotion by chanting pranav (omkar) and study good texts instructed by the sages, gain spiritual knowledge and achieve the proximity of the God.

5. Deep devotion towards God :
Saint Vyas says, "तस्मिन् परमगुरौ सर्व क्रियाणामर्पणम्'' this means, devoting all our actions to the Guru of all the Gurus, the supreme Guru, the Supreme Soul is deep devotion towards God. Only pure, auspicious and divine things can be offered to the God. Therefore, a devotee will give respect and make whole-heartedly efforts in only those things which he can offer to God and the sole aim of all his actions will be devotion to God. A true devotee always thinks that whatever he has achieved viz., body, mind, brain, strength, beauty, youth, prosperity, luxury, position, honour and entire richness is all because of the grace of God. Therefore, I should use all my energy to please the dear God. The ultimate objective of my life and efforts should be to dedicate each and everything that I have to the God, including my existence. God bestows his nectar-like-blessing on the devotees who are completely devoted to him.

Obstacles in the path of resistance towards passions :
Lot of obstacles comes in the path of such resistance towards passions and rules, which deviate us from our path. Saint Patanjali says:

वितर्कबाधने प्रतिपक्ष भावनम्

(Yogadarshan. 2/33)

While following these principles, violence, falsehood, stealing, liberal, collecting things, impurity, dissatisfaction, extravagance, irregularity in the study of Vedas, and being atheist is undutiful. One should think of its extremities and protect oneself. Having given up violence, falsehood, stealing and uncontrollable passions to protect himself from the heat of materialistic, the devotee should be determined on his decision. I have sacrificed it all and I will not embrace them again, because I did it after a serious consideration. Now I will not embrace what I have left, (like a dog who first vomits and then licks it back). I will be self-determined and follow the great rituals whole-heartedly and with full strength, this is the self duty of my life. I accept that if I have to die I will die with the hounour of fulfilling my duties.

What are these reasoning? And, what are the opposed feelings to stay safe? Saint Patanjali says in this regard-

वितर्का हिंसादय कृतकारितानुमोदिता लोभक्रोधमोहपूर्वका
मृदुमध्याधिमात्रादु खाज्ञानान्तफला इति प्रतिपक्षभावनम्

(Yogadarshan. 2/34)

This violence, untruth, stealing and other doubts which are in our inner self or those doubts which we raise through others and those which we support are caused due to greed, anger and ignorance. They have simple, medium and sharp differences and give unlimited and never ending results in the form of ignorance. This reasoning or doubt is itself an opposite feeling. Amongst these violence and reasoning, we will take the example of violence.

Types of violence against which a devotee should protect himself:

This violence is of three types. The first is the violence takes place through our mind, speech and actions. The second violence is the one which we do not do ourselves but get it done through others. And the third violence is the one for which we provoke ourselves. Being related to greed, anger and attachment, the three types of violence again have three differences. Indulging in violence by self, through others or by provoking others for flesh, skin, land, building and other greed is greed-generated violence. In the same way anger-generated violence (self, done through others or through provocation) comes with the aim of revenge. The violence generated through attachment which is done by self, through others or through provocation with the feeling that my selfish interest will be fulfilled if the selfish interests of my wife, children and other well-wishers are attained. The violence done through greed, anger or attachment is further divided into three types - polite, medium and excess.

When the extent of violence generated through anger, greed and attachment is less, it is called polite violence. If the extent is medium then the violence generated through them is also medium and if it is in excess then the violence is also in excess.

There are three stages of polite violence: 1. Extremely polite: In this case the extent of violence is extremely low. 2. Medium polite: Slightly more violent than the polite one. 3. Shrewdness: Highest state of violence in the limits of polite violence. Likewise, medium and extreme violence also have three stages each. In this way there are 81 types of violence. The 81 types of violence become manifold due to rules, alternatives and collective form. Stealing others' things and having other doubts are parts of the 81 different types of violence. Stealing, lying, unchaste life, and collecting unwanted things either done by self, through others or provoking others to do is also an obstacle for the devotee. Not speaking lies on own but making others to speak lies on your behalf and provoking others to speak lies is also untrue. In the same way, stealing, making others steal things and provoking others to steal things is all included in stealing. Leading a life of celibacy but inspiring others not to be a celibate and provoking others to be a celibate is incomplete celibacy. The same should be understood for not collecting unwanted things. As we understand for self, through others and through provocation the same should be understood with respect to lies, stealing and other greed-anger-attachment generated different types of violence and the devotee should determine in his mind that these doubts are the forms of unhappiness and give never ending results in the form of ignorance. In this way one should inculcate the feeling of reasoning, revolt towards violence, protect oneself from lies and always lead the way of yoga and rituals to meet with the individual soul.

Results of rules-resistance towards passion:
1. Result of the ritual of non-violence :

अहिंसाप्रतिष्ठायां तत्सन्निधौ वैरत्याग

(Yogadarshan. 2/35)

When a devotee has respect towards non-violence in his mind and the yogi who is in association with him, they also loose the feeling of violence and enmity. If a yogi follows the principle of non-violence through mind, speech and actions, if he is simple, pure, selfless, loving-affectionate towards all the living things, then how can it be possible for anyone to hate him? Alliance with a yogi not only removes the feeling of hatred in human beings but also in snakes, tigers and other violent wild creatures.

2. Results of good actions :

सत्यप्रतिष्ठायां क्रियाफलाश्रयत्वम्

(Yogadarshan.2/36)

The result of performing good deeds is that, whatever a yogi says it turns out to be true. A person who believes in truth, speaks and performs the same actions, his speech also becomes true. That is why the words spoken by the great people and yogis become true. It is equally important to note that yogis never speak impossible, unsuitable, and harmful words. Yogis always speak truth and tell the auspicious words. A single word of a yogi can change the whole life, and make the life flow towards auspicious world. Truthful great personalities have great power.

3. Results of not stealing others things :

अस्तेयप्रतिष्ठायां सर्वयत्नोपस्थानम्

(Yogadarshan . 2/37)

When a devotee leaves the habit of stealing other's things, he accumulates precious stones from everywhere. This is a fact that a yogi does not aspire for anything for the reason that he does not have it, leave alone the thought of stealing others things. Whatever a yogi requires to lead his life, God provides him all.

It is nature's rule that when a person has too much desire for wealth, it keep going away, and when a person rejects wealth, it comes after him. Yogis are in the same position. They are totally greedless and sensationless. Therefore the rich people from across the world provide them all types of wealth, precious stones, ornaments etc. And, yogis donates this wealth for the benefit of the mankind.

4. Results of celibacy :

ब्रह्मचर्यप्रतिष्ठायां वीर्यलाभ

(Yogadarshan. 2/38)

A yogi who leads a life of celibacy, his vigor, sharpness, shine, chastity, strength and courage increases. A person cannot become yogi when he does not lead a life of celibacy.

5. Results of renunciation

अपरिग्रहस्थैर्ये जन्मकथन्ता संबोध

(Yogadarshsn .2/39)

The result of non-acceptance of charity is that the man remains uninterested in materialism and always emerges as the winner over his senses. At that time, he gets auspicious thoughts like, who am I? Where have I come from? What should I do? A yogi is never attracted towards materialism, and through this he attains salvation by getting relieved from the bonds of life and death.

6. Results of excretion :

शौचात्स्वाङ्ग जुगुप्सा पैररसंसर्ग

(Yogadarshan. 2/40)

When devotee purifies his body with water and other things again and again, he experiences that the more he tries to purify it the more dirty and stinky it gets. It develops hatred in the person for his own body parts. And when he sees others, he finds their body dirty too and tries to avoid their touch. He hates hugging and other such acts. Saint Vyas says that-

स्थानात् बीजादुपष्ट भानिस्यन्दानिधनादपि।
कायमाधेय शौचत्वात् पण्डिता ह्यशुचिं विदु

(Yogadarshan. Vyas bhashyam)

It means that the physical body is not pure, because it comes out of impure body parts. It is made up of blood, sperm, and therefore it smells from mouth, excretory and urine place and other pores on the surface of the skin and even after death the dead body stinks a lot, therefore this body is a mass of shit. This body remains dirty in spite of purifying it with water and other things. The devotees loose interest in his body with these thoughts. He does not have any attachment with the body. He does not love the body, but the soul. This is the result of external purification. Saint Patanjali speaks about internal purification:

सत्वशुद्धिसौमनस्येकाग्रयेन्द्रियजयात्मदर्शनयोग्यत्वाति च।

(*Yogadarshan. 2/41*)

This means truth, non-violence, study of Vedas performs internal purification, happiness of the mind, concentration, victory over senses and ability to recognize the soul.

7. Results of satisfaction :

सन्तोषदनुत्तम सुखलाभ

(*Yogadarshan. 2/42*)

Happiness obtained through satisfaction is the best happiness. Happiness through satisfaction is called happiness of salvation. Saint Vyas says,

येच कामसुखं लोके यो दिव्यं महत्सुखुम्
तृष्णाक्षयसुखस्यैते नाहर्त षोडशीं कलाम्।।

This means the pleasure of sex which is compared to the heavenly happiness, is not even equal to the 1/16th part of happiness which is achieved by overcoming the desires. Therefore, there is no better form of delight than satisfaction, the desire troubles us at every step. Bhartuhari says-

तृष्णा न जीर्णा वयमेव जीर्णा, This means a person who wants his desires to be fulfilled becomes old but his desires never get old.

8. Results of ritual of devotion:

कायेन्द्रियसिद्धिरशुद्धिक्ष्या् तपस

(*Yogadarshan . 2/43*)

When the impurities destroyed with the ritual of devotion, the devotee's body and his senses become strong and healthy. Saint Dayanand Maharaj comments with respect to devotion that:

Yog Sadhna
&
Yoga Healing Secrets

"True pure feelings, belief in truth, speaking truth, not allowing the mind to follow wrong things, performing the right deeds through body, senses and mind, studying and teaching others the true Vedas, performing according to the Vedas and performing deeds of high quality are the names of devotion. Burning the humors and your skin is not called devotion.

9. Results of regular study of the Vedas :

स्वाध्यायादिष्टदेवतासंप्रयोग।

Yogadarshan. 2/44)

A yogi performing the ritual of regular study of the Vedas sees scholarly, introspecting sages and accomplished personalities and then they become helpful in his devotion. When a devotee chants omkar mantra and recites the classics of salvation and whenever he faces difficulties in devotion, accomplished holy sages guide him on his path either directly or indirectly. A devotee gets the guidance of holy preceptors according to the arrangement of God.

10. Results of deep devotion towards God :

समाधिसिद्धिरीश्वरप्रणिधानात्।

(Yogadarshan. 2/45)

This means, deep devotion towards God or devoting all the actions to the Supreme Being -God and leaving the desire to know the results of those actions, the devotee attains the stage of deep meditation very easily. ईश्वर प्रणिधानं सर्वक्रियाणांपरम गुर्वर्पणं तत्फलसंन्यासो वा। *(Vyas bhashya 2/1)* After describing the results of resistance towards passions and other rituals, we will now describe the third principle asana.

Asana :

स्थिरसुखमासनम्

(Yogadarshan. 2/46)

Sitting in padmasans, bhadrasan, sidhasan or sukhasan or any other comfortable posture is called asana. Devotee should practice to sit attentively and comfortably for a long time while doing devotion, worship and meditation, those who cannot sit in these postures and those who are sick, Saint Vyas says in their reference that, they can take the support of chairs, walls and practice pranayam-meditation etc. Posture is extremely important for devotion, meditation and worship. The spinal cord should be absolutely straight while doing any meditative worship. The surface should be even, a cushiony seat should be spread, made with *kusha* grass or blanket etc. which is a bad conductor of electricity and is comfortable. The place of worship should be secluded, having fresh air, and free of mosquitoes etc.

Today, a myth is spreading in the society that some people perform few yogasana and call themselves yogis. Yogasana is only a part of yoga principles. A person should follow the eight yogic principles including resistance towards passions, non-violence, truth, not stealing others things, celibacy and other principles and practice deep meditation for a long time with complete devotion.

Hathyoga (austerity) describes 84 different types of asanas. It describes such asanas which are related to the physical and mental health other than the meditative asanas. With the practice of these asanas, the whole body gets activated and it becomes flexible, active and healthy. Topics 5 to 10 contains complete details about useful asanas for different diseases, the readers may refer the respective pages.

Pranayam :

'तस्मिन् सति श्वासप्रश्वासयोर्गति विंछेद प्राणायाम' *(Yogadarshan. 2/49)* After accomplishment of the asanas, controlling the inhaling and exhaling of breath is called pranayam.

According to Yogadarshan there are four types of pranayam:
1.External condition 2.Internal condition 3.Stopping the breath 4.Stopping the breath while exhaling and inhaling.

बाह्या यन्तरस्त भवृत्तिर्देशकालसं याभि परिदृष्टो दीर्घसूक्ष्म। (Yogadarshan. 2/50)
बाह्या यन्तरविषयाक्षेपीश्चतुर्थ. (Yogadarshan., 2/51)

Pranayam of External condition

Method :

1. Sit in Sidhasan or Padmasan and exhale the breath as much as possible.
2. Exhale the breath and stop the breath outside by performing *moolbandh*, *uddiyan bandh* and *jalandhar bandh*.
3. When you want to breathe, remove the bandhs and inhale slowly.
4. Inhale and without stopping the breath inhale it fully. This can be done from 3 to 21 times.

Benefits :

This is a harmless pranayam. This removes the wavering of the mind. The fire of the stomach becomes illuminated. It is beneficial in stomach-related problems. The mind becomes sharp and light. This is the body purifier. It increases the speed of sperm, cures early ejaculation and nightfall and other humor related disorders.

Pranayam of Internal condition

Method :

1. Sit in a meditative posture and exhale the breath as much as possible at one instance and inhale as much as you can again. The upper portion of the chest will

be enlarged and the lower portion of the abdomen will be contracted inside. Inhale properly and perform *jalandhar bandh* and *mool bandh*.

2. Stop the breath as much as you can. When you want to exhale, remove the *jalandhar bandh* and slowly exhale.

Benefits :

It cures all the problems related to lungs. It is extremely beneficial for asthma patients. It increases vitality, vigour and shine on the body.

Stopping the breath

In this, breath has to be stopped at whatever stage it is. Stop it as long as you can and then exhale it. When the breathing is normal, stop it where ever it is. You can perform all the three bandhs in this case.

Stopping the breath while exhaling and inhaling :

Method : While exhaling, stop the breath outside in little quantity, and while inhaling stop the breath inside in little quantity. In other words when the internal air is going outside try to stop it by inhaling the outside air and when the outside air enters then push the air inside from outside and stop the outside air, in this way you have to do the opposite actions, the movement of both the air stops and the pran is in your control and the mind and senses are free. The objective of fulfilling ones duty increases and the mind becomes sharp and light and grasps any difficult or light matter very easily. The body attains increase in chastity and strengthens willpower, becomes courageous and wins over senses. Then that person can understand all the classics within a short period and produce them. The conscious becomes pure and is attentive for worship. Females can also practice yoga.

(Sa.Pra. Third stanza)

'च्योगसूत्र प्रेछर्दन विद्यारणाभ्यां वा प्राणस्यम' implies the same. We can understand it in more details. Bring the prana from upwards and apana from downwards and arrange a fight between the wind that is emitting forward (prana) and the wind that is emitting backward (apana) in the nose. In other words the air which has a tendency to remain in the heart and which moves outward bring it to the top, circulate it in the universe, bring it to the earth and establish at the center of the forehead, and the air which has a tendency to stay below the navel and try to come inside, bring it to the nostrils and establish it there. Now push both the airs and indulge them into a fight in other words do not allow the prana to go out and do not allow the outside air to enter. In this way performing opposite actions, both the airs are in your control. While performing this pranayam stabilize the mind and senses on the center portion of the forehead and concentrate your mind.

(Dhyanyoga Prakash second chapter)

Reject all the external subjects, beauty, essence, smell etc and concentrate the mind within yourself and concentrate the mind on the center portion of the forehead, i.e., in between the eyebrows. A person who normalizes both the winds moving with the help of nostrils, in other words manage the act against each other and establishing them equally is a devoted yogi, who is capable of controlling his mind, heart and senses, always aspires for salvation, free of anger and fear, he is always free.

यतेन्द्रिय मनो बुद्धिर्मुनिर्मोक्षपरायण ।
विगतेच्छाभयग्रोधो य सदा मुक्त एव स।।

(Bhagwadgita. 5/28)

The same thing has been described in the following verses.

अपाने जुह्वति प्राणं पाणेअपानं तथा परे।
प्राणापानगतीं रुद्ध्वा प्राणयाम परायणा।।
अपरेतियताहारा प्राणान् प्राणेषु जुह्वति।
सर्वेऽप्येते यज्ञविदो यज्ञाक्षयितकल्मषा।।

(Bhagwadgita 4/29-30)

These pranayams are prescribed in *Darshan Shastra* by Saint Patanjali. The internal kumbhak is included under pranayams in HathYog text for the benefit of physical, spiritual health.

सूर्यभेदनमुज्जायी सीत्कारी शीतली तथा।
भस्त्रिका भ्रामरी मूर्छा प्लाविनीत्यष्टकु भका।

(HathYog Pradipika)

The topic on Pranayam has been separated from "Yog - Its Philosophy & Practice" and published separately in a grand manner along with coloured pictures. The readers are requested to read 'Pranayam - Its Philosophy & Practice' written by respected Swamiji for the complete knowledge of pranayam.

V. *Pratyahar* (Resistance to senses) :

स्वविषयासंप्रयोगे चित्तस्वरूपानुगरइर्वनिद्रयाणां प्रत्याहार ।

(Yog Darshan. 2/54)

When the senses do not have connection with their forms and subjects then they change according to the condition of the mind, it is for this reason that when the devotee controls his mind through asceticism and wisdom, then the senses are controlled on their own, because senses carry the mind. This victory over mind and deviating from the subjects and diverting the senses and mind towards the inner self is resisting the senses. The 'hru' humor is used with reference to attraction. The opposite and prefix verb has been represented. Saint patanjali explains the results of resisting the senses:

तत परमावश्यतेन्द्रियाणाम्

(Yog Darshan, 2/55)

A devotee attains complete authority over the senses. Interest towards voice, touch, beauty, essence, and smell divert a person from the path of welfare of the soul. The interest towards each sense deviates the mind. The person who has interest towards senses is inclined towards materialistic pleasures, not in God. Therefore practice and asceticism gives the true understanding and he accomplishes resisting the senses and becomes winner over senses. Then the devotee experiences the liking, extreme happiness and satisfaction in God and the whole world appears to be unhappy.

परिणामतापसंस्कारदुखैर्गुणवृत्ति विरोद्याोच दुखमेवसर्व विवेकिन

(Yog Darshan. 2/15)

The aggregate form of all deeds result is birth, longevity and materialistic pleasure. These birth, longevity and things are full of happiness when good deeds are done and are full of unhappiness if bad deeds are done. But the worldly subjects always provide unhappiness to yogi. The reason for this is that these voice, touch, beauty and senses etc. lust for the subjects giving happiness, inspire a person towards ignorance. When you think about the results of these happiness, then we will definitely find that the worldly pleasures are also giving unhappiness because these happiness cannot be achieved without causing pain to other living things and in these happiness also the light happiness - culture and attitude have mixed unhappiness and the normal persons cannot experience them. But the yogi understands these results. Therefore, for a yogi the worldly happiness which appears to satisfy the human beings is also unhappiness.

Therefore a devotee fulfills his duty to attain God and relieve internal pain. This is external Yog from resistance to passions to resisting the senses. After this concentration, meditation and deep meditation forms of internal forms of Yog will be explained.

VI. *Dharna* (Concentration) :

देशबन्धश्चित्तस्तय धारणा

(Yog Darshan. 3/1)

Concentrating your mind on the navel center, heart which is in the form of white lotus, light glowing on your head, center of the eyebrows, front portion of the nose, front portion of the tongue and the suture on the top of the head and other physical parts and sitting at one place attentively is called concentration.

When the senses and mind starts turning inwards due to resisting the senses, concentrating them on a particular place with respect to condition is called concentration. In this way diverting the mind from a huge subject and focusing it on light aims soul-Supreme soul is called concentration. Concentration is the foundation of meditation. As the practice of concentration becomes mature, meditation also happens along with it.

VII. *Dhyan* (Meditation) :

तत्र प्रत्ययैकतानता ध्यानम्

(Yog Darshan. 3/2)

Meditation is the concentration on navel, between the eyebrows, heart etc in the form of God and having the same kind of flow with the God and solace, is meditation. As a river when it enters the sea, it intermingles with the sea. It becomes one free flow. In the same way, while meditation one should not think of anything except the Supreme Being, in other words think only of omnipresent Brahma, his enlightened quiet form and immersing in it is meditation.

Meditation is associated with every moment our lives. In Indian culture, meditation is considered to be the complete form of every action. That is the reason that today also when the elderly persons of the family direct us to do a particular task they tell us, look read carefully, walk carefully, do every work carefully. Today we use the word meditation, but what is this meditation, nobody thinks in that direction. But we can understand that the word 'meditation' is an inevitable part of our lives which is associated with every task of the world. Life is incomplete without meditation. We cannot succeed in any of the physical or spiritual objectives without meditation. We can always lead a happy and contented life only with meditation. Though meditation is a very big yogic action in itself, with which the devotees can get some guidance and directions.

Few directions or guidance for meditation :

1. Before doing meditation one should first do pranayam because pranayam makes the mind completely calm and concentrated. A calm and peaceful mind can meditate properly.

2. The mind becomes free by practicing Kapalbhati and Anulom-Vilom pranayams and the meditation takes place on its own. When the devotee performs Kapalbhati for three minutes and Anulom-Vilom pranayam for 5 to 10 minutes, then the Brahma's divine strength situated in the one of the six ganglions of the body starts moving upwards, with which all the Chakras and nerves are purified. The Supreme God starts positioning in the omkar form, heart and divine light flame. Every wavering mind also concentrates with the help of pranayam.

3. While meditating, give importance to meditation only. Do not think of anything else even if it is very auspicious at the time of meditation. Donation, service, helping others, study of Vedas, serving the teacher and serving the cow are auspicious works, but these things should not be thought of while meditation. The aim is thinking, introspecting, remembering again and again and meeting the soul and obtain God while meditating.

4. At the time of meditation make your mind introvert before meditation everyday, do not think that I am the form of nature, matter, glory. Land building, any relationship or any kind of materialistic bondage etc. This is not my expected & unexpected form. I am liberated form all the external matter or things. This body is also not my form. I am not bonded with body & senses like word, touch, form, smell. I am not the form of mind & subject of mind i.e. Anger, Passion, clout, attachment & Pride. I am liberated form Jealousies, pride, Treatment, etc. I am pure soul with bliss, and enlightenment peace. I am a son of nature. I am part of that super consciousness. Just like a drop form a ocean goes to okay and then again comes back to earth and to again merge with ocean. Drop cannot live with ocean. I am just want to be ocean of bliss from the drop. That supreme, Provides us life, power, spread, glory, peace and all the materialistic pleasure. God has provided us power birth, age, body, mind, family, parents and everything. That God is giving us all the pleasures. We are receiving external pleasures from everywhere by God. He never keeps us away form him for a moment. I am always is God and God is always in me. This synchronization always provided external bliss. God always shortness its. Continuous bliss on us. If we are not able to feel it then we are responsible for it.

5. A meditation has to live in detachment keep himself as a prime face and perform the duty of God in detached manner as a service of God. Taking pride action and expectation less work is a positive meditation of God.

6. External pleasure of medium of all pleasure seeking devices are the form of sorrow till the time we will have a pleasure oriented mind we will never indulge in a devotion,

meditation of God. And it is difficult to each the stage of super consciousness without the meditation of God.

7.	तस्य वाचक प्रणय (Yogdarshan-1/27)
तज्जपस्तदर्थभावनं (Yogdarshan -1/28)
ओमित्येकाक्षरं ब्रह्म । (Gita)
ओं खं ब्रह्म । (Yajurveda)

Beginning the meaningful chanting of Omkar is the best for meditation. God has created the eyebrows, eyes, nose, lips, ears, heart and chest and other bodily parts in the form of omkar.

This body and the entire universe are full of omkar. In this way, the devotee chants the omkar mantra and experiences The Brahma , omnipresent, spread in all places, supreme souls and merges in his divine form. Omkar is not an individual or a symbol, it is a divine power which rules the entire universe and at all places. As the soul is not visible in the body even then all the works of the body are accomplished with the existence of the soul, in the same way though in this entire universe the omkar form of Brahma is not visible to the external eyes, even then it is regulating the entire universe with its divine eyes. Along with Omkar gayatri mantra can also be chanted after understanding its meaning.

8.	The mind is concentrated by controlling the inhale and exhale and omkar should be chanted. All the senses are faulty, because the eyes can see good and bad things, ears can listen descent and indecent things, nose can smell fragrance and odour, speech can say both true or lies, tongue eats both digestible and indigestible things, mind develops both good and bad thoughts therefore any form is not completely flawless. Life is completely free of faults and without shape. Therefore to meet the flawless and shapeless Brahma we should take the shelter of flawless life and chant omkar. Whenever you get time, look within yourself and take long and short breaths and with every exhalation chant omkar. The speed of inhaling and exhaling should be so slow that one should not be able to listen to himself and a cotton piece kept in front the nostril also should not move. Try to inhale and exhale once in one minute. In this way try to see the breath inside. In the beginning the touch of breath will be felt at the front portion of the nose. Gradually you will experience the touch of deep breath as well. In this way chanting omkar along with looking within yourself, meditation is achieved on its own. This is normal Yog and while meditation the devotee sees the God within himself and attains the happiness of deep meditation. The devotee should do the same before going to bed, this makes the sleep also full of Yog. With this practice the entire life of devotee becomes full of Yog.

9. In this way every person aspiring for salvation should meditate at least for an hour everyday and perform devotion, worship and meditation. If this is done all the worries of this world are destroyed and we experience the supreme soul -God. We should always remember that the sole aim of life is meeting with the individual soul and obtaining God, rest everything is secondary. If we do not start walking on the path of meeting with the soul, then sage in Upanishad's says, "pride is perishable". Therefore Yog and meditation are the necessities of our lives.

VIII. *Samadhi* (Union with the Infinite) :

तदेवार्थमात्रनिर्भासं स्वरुपशून्यमिव समाधि।

(Yog Darshan. 3/3)

When the meditation is in the form of God or a hollow like the light which illuminates our form, then it is called deep meditation.

The devotee gets so engrossed, merges and gets lost in the blissful, enlightened and peaceful form of God while chanting omkar that he forgets himself, he only experiences the divine form of God. He merges with the Supreme Soul. Immortal great saint Dayansand Maharaj says that the only difference between meditation and deep meditation is that in case of meditation, the mediator, the mind with which he is meditating and the thing for which he is meditating are all present. But in case of deep mediation, only the happy, enlightened and peaceful form of God and divine-knowledge-enlightened soul merges with it, here there is no difference in the three aspects. As a person dips in the water and stays there for a while, in the same way the individual soul merges with God and experiences the bliss of deep meditation. The same thing, sages narrate in a different way like the iron when thrown in fire takes the form of fire in the same way the soul should be enlightened in the divine knowledge of God and forget ourselves and completing ourselves in the light and happy form of God and accomplish ourselves with complete knowledge is called deep meditation. Shri Bhojaraj says with reference to deep meditation:

सम्यगाधीयत एकाग्री क्रियते विक्षेपान् परिहृत्य मनो यत्र स समाधि ।

This means the stage when the mind is diverted from doubts and only the truth is grasped, in other words concentration is achieved, that is called deep meditation. The stage which includes doubts and queries described in the first stanza of *Yogdarshan* should be considered to be a single stage of meditation because they have words, meaning, knowledge and alternatives. And the stage without doubts and queries should be considered as deep meditation. This contemplation of mind is the highest level of deep meditation and in this stage the devotee obtains the knowledge in the form of *prasada*. After this deep meditation also a high level - this is meaningless, without anything. In this stage of deep meditation the lust or desires for things of pleasure also does not exist in the mind. The impressions completely destroy along with the seed, all the conditions of the mind come to an end. Then the possibility of falling in the worldly bonds also destroys, this is called contemplation of the highest order. This is perfection of Yog or life , by obtaining it a yogi in the words of Saint Vyas says:

प्राप्तं प्रापणीयं, क्षीणा क्षेतव्या, छिन्न शिलष्टपर्वा भवसंक्रम।
यस्याविच्छेदाजनित्वा म्रियते मृत्वा च जायत इति। ज्ञानस्यैव पराकाष्ठग
वैराग्यम्। एतस्यैव हि नान्तरीयकं कैवल्यमिति।।

(Yog Darshan. Vyasbhashyam 1/16)

The meaning of this is, the last limit of knowledge is asceticism. Reaching this highest stage with deep meditation definitely leads to the salvation of the soul, by which the yogi feels that he has achieved everything in his life, the ignorance and other sufferings (ignorance, pride, jealousy, hatred and attachment) are destroyed. Whose organs are joined, and the entry of a soul in other body is disintegrated, due to which a creature takes birth and dies and takes rebirth after death. This is the short description of deep meditation.

(Light) Exercises

Following are some light exercises for the healthy joints and to provide strength, activity and health to the nervous system

Sitting position in Dandasan :

Process :

All the asanas, which are done by sitting are begun with the condition of Dandasan. Both the legs should be straight in the front. Both the hands should rest on the ground on both the sides, the fingers turned backwards and the hands and back should be straight.

Practice steps :

1. **For the toes :** slowly press the toes and big toes of both the legs forwards applying force. The same should be repeated backwards as well. The ankles should be firm. Repeat this eight to ten times.

2. **Ankles and legs :** join both the legs and press the ankles and paws forward gently in forward and backward direction. The ankle will have friction with the ground. This practice is beneficial for sciatica pain and knees.

3. **For the paws :** Keep both the legs at a distance. First turn the paw of the right leg in circular motion and make a circle with the paws. Repeat this five to seven times. Then do the same in opposite direction. In the same way practice with the other leg and then with both the legs.

4. **For knees and hips :** fold the right leg and put it on the left thigh. Catch the right paw with left hand and keep the right hand on the right knee. Now, keep the right hand under the right knee take the knee upwards towards the chest and while pressing bring it down and rest it on the ground. In the same way continue the exercise by keeping the left paw on the right thigh and repeat as mentioned above. In end catch both the paws with both the hands and rest them on the ground and lift them up. In this way make semi- circular portions many times (butterfly). This is a good exercise to reduce the fat in the hip area and make the hip joint healthy. This will help in sitting in Padmasan as well.

5. For the knees : (1) Keeping the legs straight, keep both the hands on the sides of the waist. Press and leave the knee, joint do the action of contraction and expansion. After this join the fingers of both the hands and place them under the knee and catch the thigh. Then fold the leg and bring it near the hips and do the action of cycling and make a circle from the front direction with the leg. In the same way repeat it with the other leg.

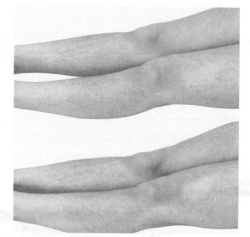

2) Stand straight, bring both the ankles and the knees togeth on the knees and first with the left and then with the right k motion. Repeat this exercise five to seven times. This exer knees.

6. For the stomach and waist (Grinding) : 1) Interlock the fingers of both the hands and keep them in front of both the legs. Turn the hands from left to right in such a way that the waist bends forward and while touching the toes with the hands rotate them in a circular motion. When the hands reach the thighs then move the waist backwards. Keep the legs straight. In the same way repeat the exercise from the other side.

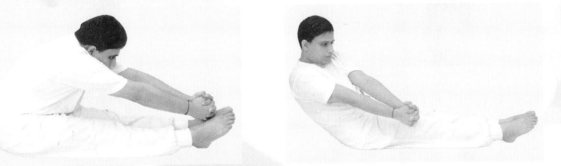

2) Stretch both legs wide apart in the front. Bring both the hands and lift upwards in the same level. Then catch the big toe of the left leg with the right hand and turn the left hand in an upward direction and keep it straight, turn the neck backwards and look back. In the same way repeat the exercise with the left hand. Both the exercises strengthen the stomach and relieve the backache and reduce the fat accumulated on the waist; but those who have severe backache should not do these exercises.

7. For the back : Catch the wrists with opposite hands and lift them and take them at the back of the head. Inhale and pull the left hand with the right hand from the back of the head. The head and neck should be straight. Then exhale and take the hands upwards. In the same way repeat the exercise with the other hand.

8. For the fingers of the hands : 1) Stretch both the hands forwards and bring them to the level of the hands and keep the paws down. Then slowly press the finger tips applying force and straighten them.2) After this fold the big finger and press the fingers making a fist like shape and slowly open it. Repeat this 10 to 12 times.

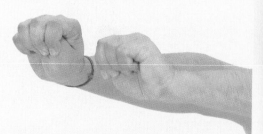

Yog Sadhna
&
Yoga Healing Secrets

9. For hands and cervical sodalities and frozen shoulders :

Fold the big finger and press it with the fingers, close the fists and bring them straight to the shoulder level and turn both the fists in circular motion in both the directions. The elbows should be straight.

10. For the elbow : 1) Bring both the palms upwards and stretch the hands straight. Now, fold the elbow and touch the shoulders with the fingers. Then slowly straighten them. 2) The same exercise should be repeated backwards by keeping both the hands at the level of the shoulders at both sides.

11. For heart, cervical and shoulder pain :

1) Fold both the hands and keep them on the shoulders. Keep the elbows in the front at the level of the shoulders. Then join both the elbows and bring them near the chest and rotate them in circular motion and make a big circle. Repeat this exercise in the opposite direction as well.

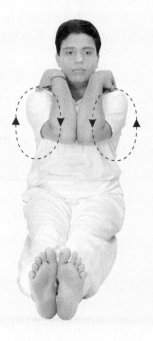

2) Fold the fists of both the hands and bring it near the chest in such a manner that the back side of the fingers should touch each other. Now inhale, open the hands slowly in the front, but keep it in mind that the fingers should join each other in a proper manner, they should not be separate. While keeping the hands straight, exhale and bring the hands to the chest. Repeat this several times.

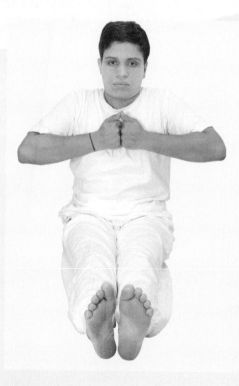

12. For the neck: 1)

Sit straight and rotate the neck right and touch it to the right shoulder. In the same way repeat it for the left shoulder. After this bend the neck forward and touch the chest with the chin and slowly take it backwards and bend backwards as much as you can. In the end rotate the neck in circular motion in both the directions.

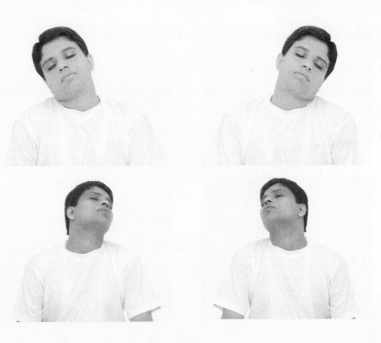

2) Keep the right hand on the right portion of the head above the ear and press the hand with the head. In this way press the head with hand and hand with head against each other, this causes vibration in the neck. Repeat this four to five times and repeat this exercise from the left side as well.

3) Interlock the fingers of both the hands and press the hands with the head and the head with both the hands. While doing this the neck and head should be straight, pressing hand and head against each other will cause vibration in the neck which is beneficial for the health of the neck and the blood circulation will be proper.

13. For the eyes :

Keep the neck straight and rotate the pupils of the eyes upward-downward and then left to right and then right to left and then in a circular motion.

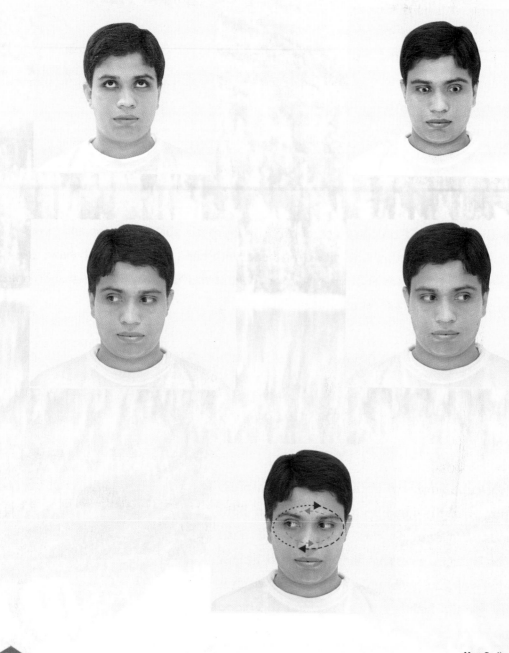

Yog Sadhna
&
Yoga Healing Secrets

Rules useful for the Asanas

1. Time : Asanas can be done in the morning and evening. If you cannot do it both the times, morning is best. The mind remain calm in the morning. Asanas can be done in the morning after performing daily chores and with empty stomach or after 5 to 6 hours after lunch in the evening. One should be free of any excretion before doing asana. If there is a problem of constipation then one should drink water kept in a copper or silver glass in the morning. After this one should take a stroll. The stomach gets cleaned. If it is a severe case of constipation then before going to bed one should take *triphala* powder with warm water.

2. Place : Pure, calm and secluded place is best for asanas. It greenery of trees, park, garden, pond, river side are best available places. Required oxygen is available in open areas and near the trees, which is beneficial for the health. If asanas and pranyanam are being done at home, then light a *diya* or *guggul* and fill the air with perfume.

3. Clothes : while doing asanas clothes should be minimum possible and comfortable. Males can wear half pant and banian. Ladies can wear salwar, blouse etc. and do pranayam and other asanas.

4. Cushion and quantity : It is better to spread a soft mat or blanket on the ground. Do not do asanas in open areas. Do the asanas according to your ability. The asanas which are practiced for one hour are considered to be complete, medium practice in 30 minutes and short practice in 15 minutes.

5. Age : concentrate the mind, be cheerful and enthusiastic and practise it according to your mind and physical strength. Only then the person can achieve the benefits of yoga. Weak and old people should do asanas in limited number. Children above the age of 10 can do all the exercises. Pregnant ladies should not attempt difficult exercises. They should do the exercise slowly, taking long breath, chanting Omkar and Gayarti mantra and meditating.

6. Stage/age and cautions : The asana and pranayam can be done in any stage. By performing such acts healthy person become more healthy. He does not become sick and sick person become healthy. Even then there are few asanas which a sick person should not perform, for example, whose ears secret, eyes are red, the nervous system and the heart is weak, they should not perform Shirshasan. Weak heart people should not perform heavy exercises like full Shalabhasan, Dhanurasan, etc. Persons suffering with hernia should not do asanas which put pressure on the lower part of the navel. Patients of high blood pressure should not do Shirshasan and other exercises which put strain on the head and the ladies should not perform exercises during the five days of menstrual cycle. Those who have pain in the neck and back should not do exercises, in which they have to bend forward.

7. Food : Food should be taken after half an hour of asanas. Food should include pious items. Fried and spicy food items should not be consumed, which causes stomach disorder. One should not drink tea after asanas, having tea once destroys around 50 cells of liver and other delicate glands. With this you can imagine that tea is very harmful. This is also a bitter enemy of health, which deforms the holy body which is a form of temple. It has some sort of alcohol which makes the person addicted to it. It reduces the fire of the stomach, causes acidity, gas, constipation and other problems arise and tea is the biggest contributor to all these problems. Tea and allopathic medicines are the two main factors, which have a major role in deforming the liver.

8. Inhale - exhale rules : While doing asanas it is a normal rule to exhale while bending forward and inhale while moving backwards. Respiration should be done through nostrils only, not with mouth, because respiration done through nose filters the air and then passes it inside.

9. Sight : Asanas done with closed eyes increases concentration, which eliminates mental stress and inattentiveness. Normally asanas and pranayam can be done with eyes open.

10. Steps: Some asanas have to be done both the sides. If an asana has been done by lying to the right side, then it should be done on the other side as well. Other than this, fix the number of repetitions of each asana to be done so that the exercises of the muscles and joints are completed in the opposite direction. For example, one should do Matsyasan, Mandukasan and Sarvangasan after Ushtrasan. The beginners will experience pain in the muscle and joints for the first two to four days. Continue the practice. The pain will relieve on its own. Whenever you get up after doing the asanas in lying position you should also do the asanas by bending to the left side. At the end of practice, Shavasan should be done for 8 to 10 minutes, so that the body organs are relaxed.

11. Rest : Whenever you feel tired while doing asanas, at that time Shavasan and Makarasan should be done to rest the body. When you are tired you can rest in the middle of the practice as well.

12. Religious instructor : Yoga is accomplished with the grace of religious instructor and by following the path as directed by him. Therefore, yoga asanas, pranayam, meditation should be practiced under the supervision of a religious instructor.

13. Resistance towards passion and rules : the yoga practitioners should follow the principle of resistance towards passion and rules with complete strength and will power. Without following these principles nobody can become a yogi.

14. Temperature of the body : If the body temperature is very high or if there is fever, in such a situation if the body temperature increases on doing asanas, then inhale through left nostril and exhale through the right nostril. This should be repeated several times and bring the temperature to normal.

15. Cleaning the stomach : If the stomach does not get cleaned, there can be constipation or problem of digestion, then in the beginning for few days some soft *harad* or *tripahals* etc., should be taken before going to bed. In the situation where the stomach does not get cleaned, there can be problem in eyes, mouth, head, weak nervous system etc. Therefore it is necessary for the stomach to get cleaned, without constipation, without indigestion, taking proper sleep during the night and take proper diet and sexual pleasure.

16. Difficult asanas : A person whose bone is fractured any time, they should not practice difficult asanas, other wise the bone can break again at the same place.

17. When it sweats : If it sweats at the time of asanas, it should be wiped with a towel, this refreshes the body, the skin remains healthy and the bacteria do not enter the body. Yogasanas should be practiced according to ability after getting freed from bath etc. After 15 to 20 minutes of exercise bath can be taken when the temperature becomes normal.

Main asana for Stomach problem, diabetes, obesity

The asanas which have been described here, all are useful for the stomach especially Along with the stomach these asanas have other benefits which have been mentioned at the respective places. The word 'stomach' brings to our mind the entire digestive system, which includes stomach, liver, spleen, intestines, abdomen and gall bladder and fire of the stomach. We have written earlier also that fluid and blood are produced when the food is digested through the digestive system. Therefore these asanas will provide complete physical benefit to the person. the health of the heart also depends on the digestive system. The patients of heart problem normally have the problem of indigestion, gas is produces which affects the heart and the heart beat increases due to gas and wind related problems. Therefore these asana are useful for the heart patients as well.

Sarvangasan :

Sarvangasan

Method:

1. Lie down straight on your back. The legs should be together, join the hands to the sides and rest the palms on the ground.

2. Inhale and raise the legs at 30 degrees upwards, then 60 degrees and then 90 degrees. You can support the back while lifting the legs. If the legs cannot be kept straight at 90 degrees take them back at 120 degrees and rest the hands at the back. The elbows should rest on the ground. The paws should be straight the eyes should be closed otherwise glance at the toes. In the beginning it can be done for 2 minutes and then slowly increase the time up to half an hour.

3. While coming back keep the legs straight and bend backwards slightly. Remove both the hands from the back and rest them straight on the ground. Now, press the floor with the palms and get up in the same position as you had lied down, first back and then the legs should be laid straight on the floor. The duration for Sarvangasan

and Shavasan should be the same. The reverse asanas for these is Matsyasan. Therefore, performing Matsyasan before Shavasan is more beneficial.

Benefits :

1. It activates the thyroid and makes it healthy. This reduces obesity, weakness, increases the height and tiredness etc. It strengthens the adrenal glands, semen glands and ovaries.

2. Other benefits are similar to Shavasan. But the specialty of this asana is that those patients for whom Shavasan is restricted, they can also do this asana. It is beneficial for two to three stages of asthma because the shoulders are straight in this asana. Respiration is also abdominal. The weight of the stomach, intestines etc, falls on the abdominal muscles and thereby the diaphragm gets toned due to participation in the inhale and exhale process.

3. This is beneficial for increasing height as it activates the thyroid and pituitary glands.

Uttanapadasan

Method:

1. Lie down straight on your back . Palms towards the ground, legs straight and paws together.

2. Inhale and raise the legs straight upwards up to 30 degrees and till some time be in the same position.

3. While coming down slowly rest the legs on the floor and not suddenly. After resting for a while repeat the exercise. Do it 3 to 6 times.

4. Those who have backache, they should do it with single leg.

Uttanapadasan

Benefits :

1. This asana strengthens the intestines and makes them disease free. It cures constipation, gas, obesity and increases the fire of the stomach.

2. It is useful in shifting of the navel, heart problem, stomach pain, and respiratory problems.

3. It is especially useful when done with lifting single leg.

Halasan

Method :

1. Lie down straight on your back, inhale and slowly lift the legs. First 30 degrees, then 90 degrees and then take the legs at the back of the head and then lift the back also and exhale.

2. Rest the legs on the backside on the floor. Let the breathing be normal. In the beginning the hands can be used to support the back for comfort. In the completion stage keep the hands on the floor, stay in this position for 30 seconds.

3. While coming back follow the same steps as used while going up, rest the hands on the press the floor with palms and straighten the legs and rest the knees on the ground.

Halasan

Benefits:

1. The spine is healthy and flexible and the back muscles become extended and disease free.

2. It activates the thyroid glands and reduces obesity, stunted growth and weakness.

3. It is beneficial in indigestion, dysentery, gas, constipation, spleen and liver disorders and heart disease.

4. It activates the pancreas and reduces diabetes.

5. It is beneficial in painful menstruation and gynecological problems.

Cautions:

1. This asana should not be done incase of enlarged liver, spleen.

2. Patients of high blood pressure, cervical and spinal problems should not do this asana.

3. In case of slip disc and tuberculosis of spine the asana should not be done.

Karna Pidasan

Method :

Like Halasan rest the legs at the back of the head and bend both the knees and bring them near the ears. The remaining method is same like Halsasan.

Karna Pidasan

Benefits :

All the benefits are same like Halasan. It is especially beneficial in ear problems, that is why it has been named Karnapidasan.

Naukasan

Method :

1. Keep both the hands on the thighs and lie down straight. Inhale and first raise the head and shoulders upwards and then the legs. The legs, hands and head should be lifted at the same level like a boat.

2. Stay for a while in this position and slowly bring down the hands, legs and head to the floor while exhaling. In this way rotation can be done three to six times. The reverse asana for this Dhanurasan. This implies that Dhanurasan should be done after Naukasan.

Naukasan

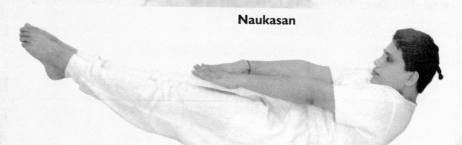

Benefits :

1. The benefits are same as of Uttanapadasan.
2. The lungs and heart become strong due to the entry of prana.
3. It is beneficial for intestines, stomach, liver and pancreas.

Pavan Muktasan

Method:

1. Lie down straight and rest the right knee on the chest.
2. Interlock both the hands and keep them on the knee, while exhaling press the knee and rest it on the chest and while lifting the leg touch the knee with the nose. Remain in this position for about 10 to 30 seconds while stopping the air outside and then lie down straight. Repeat this two to four times.

Pavan Muktasan (1)

3. In the same way do the exercise with the other leg. In the end practice this asana with both the legs. This completes one rotation. Repeat this three to four times.

Pavan Muktasan (2)

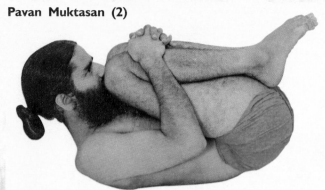

4. Hold both the legs and do the massage of the back. Bend forward, backward, right-left while remaining in this position.

Benefits :

1. This asana gives benefits as per its name. It is extremely beneficial for wind related stomach problems.
2. It is beneficial for gynecological problems, mild menstruation, painful menstruation and uterus related diseases.
3. It is beneficial in acidity, heart disease, gout and backache.
4. It reduces the fat on the stomach.
5. If there is severe pain in the back, then lift the head and touch the knee with the nose. Press only the legs and bring them to the chest. In this way slip disc, sciatica and backache are cured.

Kandharasan

Method :

1. Lie down straight, fold the knees and keep the legs near the hips.

2. Hold the upper portion of the ankle with hands..

3. Inhale and raise the back and hips. The shoulders and ankles should rest on the ground. Stay in this position for 15 to 20 minutes.

4. While coming down exhale and slowly rest the back on the floor. Repeat this 3 to 4 times

kandharasan

Benefits :

1. It is best to keep the navel in its position. It is beneficial for stomach pain, backache.

2. It is especially beneficial for uterus. It cures infertility, menstrual disorder, white discharge, bleeding and humor related problems in males.

Padangushthasparshasan

Method :

1. Lie down straight and bend the right leg and hold the feet with both the legs and while exhaling pull the leg, lift the head and touch the nose with the big toe.

Padangushthasparshasan (1)

Yog Sadhna
&
Yoga Healing Secrets

2. In the same way practice with the left leg and in the end do the exercise with the both the legs.

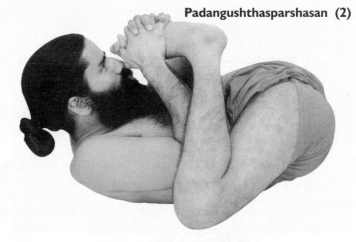

Padangushthasparshasan (2)

Benefits :

1. This is an important exercise to rectify the navel . When the navel is rectified, it cures gas, stomach pain, constipation, dysentery, weakness and laziness.

2. It is beneficial for pancreas, stomach and intestines.

Dirgha Naukasan

Method :

1. Lie sown in Shavasan and straighten both the hands while taking them at the back of the head.

2. Inhale, slowly raise the legs, head and hands at least one foot above the ground level and the hips and the lower portion of the back should rest on the ground. The vision should be at the chest. While coming down, exhale and slowly rest the hands, legs and head on the floor.

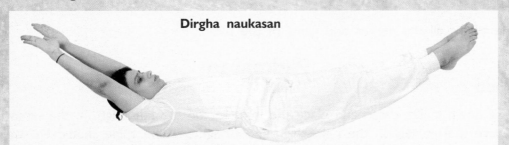

Dirgha naukasan

Benefits :

1. It is beneficial for the stomach and back just like Naukasan.

2. It is the best asana to strengthen the heart, therefore it is also called Hridayastambhasan.

3. Females should definitely do this exercise except during pregnancy. This gives good shape to their body and it becomes active.

Prishtatanasan

Method :

1. Lie down on your stomach. Stretch the hands straight in the front and keep the hands on the top of each other while putting the palms on the floor.

2. The legs should be straight and the paws should be at the back. The forehead should rest between both the hands.

3. Inhale and pull the hands forward and stretch the legs backwards. Practice this asana by keeping the body straight. This will cause vibration in the back. Exhale and relax the body. Repeat this three to four times.

Prishtatanasan

Benefits :

It strengthens all the nerves and veins of the back.

Padmasan

Method :

1. Sit down in Dandasan and place the right leg on the left thigh. In the same way place the left leg on the right thigh and straighten. The spine should be straight. As per convenience, place the left leg on the right thigh and firmly place the right leg on the left thigh.

2	Keep the right hand below the left hand and place them on the lap (anjali), focus the mind on the front portion of the nose or any other center and meditate the name of God.

3.	In the beginning practice this for one or two minutes. Gradually increase the time.

Benefits :

1.	This is the best asana for meditation. It is helpful in concentration of the mind and lifting the prana.

2.	It increases the fire of the stomach. It is beneficial in wind related problems.

Padmasan

Badhpadmasan

Badhpadmasan
Method:

1. Sit in Padmasan, fold the left hand bring it from the backside and touch the big toe of the left leg and in the same way bring the right hand from the backside and touch the big toe of the right leg.

2. The spine and back should be straight. Close the eyes and try to concentrate the mind.

Benefits :

1. It increases the chest of males and females and makes it beautiful.

2. It is beneficial for hands, shoulders, and the entire back area.

Yoga Mudrasan (1)

Method :

1. Sit in Padmasan and keep the palm of the right hand on the navel and keep the left palm on the right hand. While exhaling bend forwards and rest the chin on the floor. Look straight.

2. While inhaling come back to normal position. Repeat this four to five times.

Yoga Mudrasan (1)

Benefits :

1. It is best exercise for stomach. It increases the fire of the stomach and cures gas, indigestion and constipation.

2. It is extremely beneficial for activating the pancreas and controlling diabetes.

Yoga Mudrasan (2)

Method :

1. Sit in Padmasan and take both the hands backward and hold the left wrist with the right hand.

2. While exhaling rest the chin on the floor, look straight. If the chin does not rest on the ground, then bend forwards as much as possible.

Yoga Mudrasan (2)

Benefits : Same as above.

Yog Sadhna
&
Yoga Healing Secrets

Matsyasan

Method :

1. Sit in Padmasan and taking the support of both the hands, bend backwards and rest the elbows on the ground.

2. While resting the palms on back of the shoulders, with their support bend the neck backwards as much as you can. The back and chest should be above the ground level and rest the knees on the floor.

3. Hold the toes with the elbows and rest them on the floor. Inhale and stop the breath.

Matsyasan

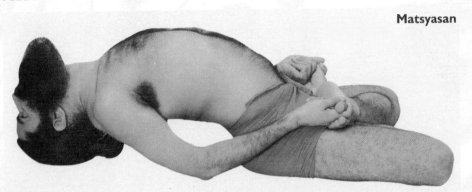

4. While leaving the asana come back to the normal position as done in the beginning or straighten the legs while resting the shoulders and head on the ground and lie down in Shavasan.

5. This is the reverse asana for Sarvangasan. Therefore it should be done after Sarvangasan.

Benefits :

1. This is the best exercise for stomach. It activates the intestines and cures constipation.

2. It makes the thyroid, parathyroid and adrenal glands healthy.

3. It is beneficial in case of cervical or when the back bone is enlarged.

4. It stops the shifting of the navel. It cures lungs diseases, asthma and other respiratory troubles.

Vajrasan

Method :

1. Fold both the legs and place them under the hips in such a way that the ankles are protruding out and the paws are near the hips.

2. In this position the big toes of both the legs will be together. The back, neck and the head should be straight. Knees should be joined together. Keep the hands on the knees.

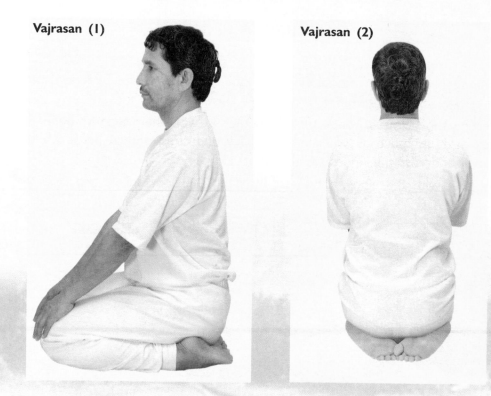

Vajrasan (1)   Vajrasan (2)

Benefits :

1. It is a meditative asana. It removes the inattentiveness of the mind.

2   This is the only asana which can be done after meals. This exercise cures indigestion, acidity, gas, constipation. The food digestion becomes normal when this asana is done for 5 to 15 minutes after meals. Otherwise in normal yoga practice, it should be done for 1 to 3 minutes.

Suptavajrasan

Method :

1. Sit in Vajarasan and keep the hands on the backside and with their support bend the body backwards and rest the head on the ground. The knees should be together and resting on the ground.

2. Slowly try to rest the neck, shoulders and back also on the ground. Keep the hands straight on the thighs.

3. While leaving the asana, sit in Vajrasan while taking the support of hands and elbows.

Suptavajrasan

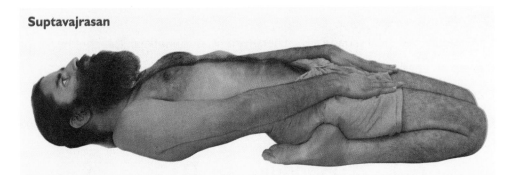

Benefits :

1. In this asana the lower part of the stomach stretches which activates the large intestine and reduces constipation.

2. Shifting of navel rectifies and it is beneficial for the kidneys.

Shashakasan

Method :

1. Sit in Vajrasan and while inhaling lift both the hands upwards.

2. Bend forwards and exhale and stretch both the hands forward and place the palms on the ground and rest the hands on the ground. The forehead should also rest on the ground.

3. Stay in this position for some time and again come back in Vajrasan.

Shashakasan

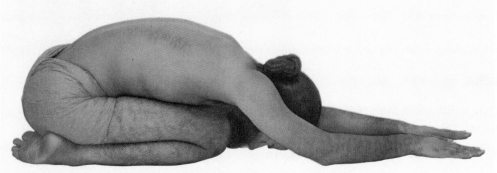

Benefits :

1. It massages the heart naturally. Therefore it is beneficial for the heart patients.

2. It gives strength to the pancreas, intestines, liver and kidneys.

3. It cures mental illness, stress, anger, irritation etc.

4. It strengthens the uterus in females. It reduces the fat from stomach, waist and buttocks.

Mandukasan (1)

Method :

1. Sit in Vajrasan and close the fists of the both the hands. While pressing the fists fold the big finger inside and press inside.

2. Pressing the navel with both the fists exhale and bend forward. Look straight.

3. Stay in this position for some time and come back to Vajrasan. Repeat this 3 to 4 times.

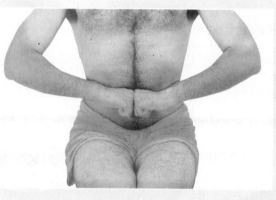

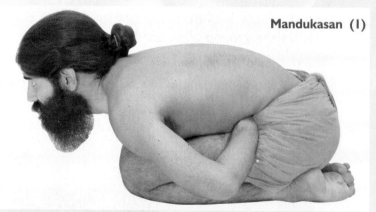

Mandukasan (1)

Benefits :

1. It activates the pancreas. Therefore the insulin is produced in large quantity. It is beneficial in curing diabetes.

2. It is beneficial in stomach problems.

3. It is beneficial for the heart.

Mandukasan (2)

Method :

Sit in Vajrasan and place the left palm on the right palm and keep them on the navel and press inwards and while exhaling bend forwards like Mandukasan(1). Repeat this three to four times.

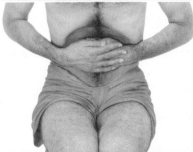

Mandukasan (2)

Benefits :

As mentioned above.

Kurmasan

Method :

1. Sit in Vajrasan and place the elbows on both sides of the navel. Keep the palms up and join the hands and keep them straight.

2. While exhaling bend forwards. Touch the chin with the palms. Look straight. While inhaling come back to original position or while breathing normally stay in that position for a minute.

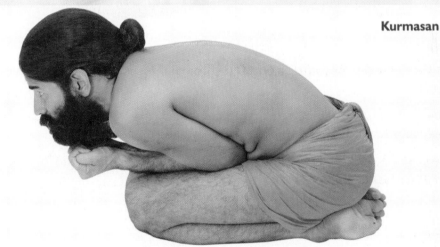

Kurmasan

Benefits : As mentioned above.

Paschimottanasan

Method :

1. Sit in Dandasan and hold the toes with the help of big and index fingers of the hands.

2. Exhale and bend forwards and try to place the head in between the knees. The stomach can be kept in the position of *Uddiyan bandh*. The knees and legs should rest on the ground and the elbows should also rest on the ground. Remain in this position for half to three minutes according to capacity. While exhaling come back to normal position.

3. After this asana the reverse asanas Bhujangasan and Shalabhasan should be done.

Paschimottanasan

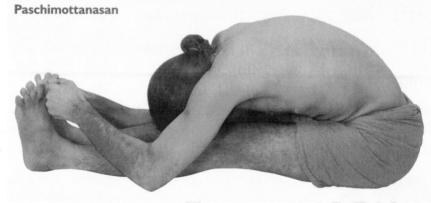

Benefits :

1. All the back muscles become strong. The stomach muscles contract. This increases their health.

2. According to Hathpradipika this asana inspires the prana towards the three principle nerves with which the kundalini awakes.

3. It increases the fire of the stomach and cures the sperm related problems. It is an important asana for increasing the height.

Vakrasan

Method :

1. Sit in Dandasan and bend the right leg and place it close to the knee of the left thigh. Keep the left leg straight.

2. Keep the left hand between the right leg and the stomach and rest it near the left leg paw.

3. Keep the right hand at the back and rest it straight on the ground. Turn the neck to the right and see, keep the left leg, waist, right hand straight. Repeat this four to six times.

4. The same should be done in the other direction.

Vakrasan

Benefits :

1. This reduces the fat from the waist. It is beneficial for the liver and the spleen.

Ardhamtsyendrasan

Method :

1. Sit in Dandasan and fold the left leg and place the ankle near the hips.

2. Place the right leg near the left knee towards outside on the ground.

3. Hold the left paw with the left hand while keeping it near the left knee towards outside.

4. Fold the right hand backwards and look back

5. The same should be repeated for the other side.

Ardhamtsyendrasan

Benefits :

1 It is beneficial in diabetes and backache.

2. It regulates the blood circulation in all the nerves and veins situated near the spine.

3. It cures the stomach disorders and strengthens the intestines.

Purna Matsyendrasan

Method :

Purna Matsyendrasan

1. Sit in the above mentioned position and fold the left leg and place it close to the navel above the right thigh and fold the right leg and place it near the left knee with the paw straight.

2. While keeping the left hand near the right knee towards outside hold the right toe or paw.

3. Keep the right hand at the back on the floor.

4. Remain in this position for half to three minutes.

5. This asana should be done on both right and left sides.

Benefits : As mentioned above.

Gomukhasan

Gomukhasan

Method :

1. Sit in Dandasan and fold the left leg and place the ankle near the left hip, other wise you can also sit on the ankle.

2. Fold the right leg and place it above the left leg in such a way that both the knees should touch each other.

3. Lift the right hand and bend it back and take the left hand to the back and hold the right hand. Keep the neck and back straight.

4. Do this for one minute from one side and repeat the same with the other side.

Benefits :

1. It is extremely beneficial in hydrosol and enlargement of the intestines.

2. It is beneficial in humor related problems, diabetes and gynecological problems.

3. It strengthens the liver, kidney and the chest. It cures arthritis and gout.

Pashuvishramasan

Process :

1. Sit in Dandasan and fold the left leg in such a way that the paw is towards outside and the ankle is touching the hips.

2. Fold the right leg and place the paw near the left thigh.

3. While inhaling lift both the hands upwards and while exhaling bend forwards, the head and hands should rest on the ground. While inhaling again lift the hands and while exhaling bend towards the left side. While bending forwards and lifting up keep the hands straight while touching the ears.

4. In the same way change the leg and repeat the exercise on the other side.

Pashuvishramasan

Benefits :

It reduces the fat accumulated at the back of the waist. It is beneficial in diabetes and stomach problems.

Janushirasan

Process :

1. Sit in Dandasan and fold right leg and place the paw near the beginning of the left thigh and place the ankle near the mid portion of the genitals and rectum.

2. Hold the paw of the left leg with both the hands and while exhaling rest the head on the knees and wait in this position for some time and then while inhaling get up and repeat the exercise with the other leg.

Janushirasan

Benefits: Same as for Paschimottanasan.

Exercise for relaxation:
Shavasan (Yoganidra)

Shavasan

Lie down straight with your back on the ground. Keep a distance of one foot between the legs and keeping both the hands little further from the thighs, keep the hands slightly open towards upward direction. Close the eyes, neck straight, the whole body should be relaxed. Slowly take four to five deep breaths and leave. Now, look at each part of the body through your mind with determination and experience that each organ is in relaxed condition and tension free. Determination is the force behind all the works and great objectives. Now we have to give complete rest to our body. For this also we have to take the determination of relaxing and resting the body.

First and foremost, with the determination of the mind look at the toes of legs leave them totally loose and tension free. After toes look at the ankles experience their relaxation. Now see the calf muscles and think that my calf muscles are absolutely healthy, tension free and in the position of total rest and experience that the whole body is getting rest by the mere feeling of relaxation. As we start crying with the feeling of extreme sorrow, we laugh with the feeling of happiness, and the blood starts boiling with the mere feeling of victory, in the same way the body starts experiencing total rest only with the mere feeling of relaxation. After calf muscles now looking at the knees, experience that they are healthy, and in the condition of tension free. Within the mind look at the thighs and experience them to be in the condition of total rest. After thighs gradually look at the upper parts of the body-waist, stomach, back, looking at them with ease experience the situation of total rest, health and tension free. Now with quiet feeling concentrate the mind on the heart and try to listen to the heart beats. Listen to the divine tune of the heart and think that my heart is absolutely healthy, tension free and in the situation of total rest, there is no disorder or disease in my heart. Now relaxing the lungs and the heart, look at the shoulders and experience them to be in the situation of tension free and totally relaxed. Then look at hands, elbows, wrists and fingers of both the hands and big fingers and experience the hands to be in the situation of tension free, relaxed, and total rest.

Now look at the face and think there is no worry, tension, disappointment or any negetive feeling on my face. There is happiness, gladness, expectation and calmness on my face. There is unlimited happiness on my face including my eyes, nose, ears. Till now we have given total rest to the body with the determination and thought of good things. Now we have to give total rest to the mind and relax the mind. Now we have to move away from the thoughts arising in the mind. For this we have to take the shelter of the soul. Think that - I am the son of the soul which is always pure-hearted, clean, pious, calm, happy, and enlighten nectar. I am always complete and immortal. I do not lack anything, in fact I am always full of feelings and devotion. I am the part of the happy form of the God. I am the nectar son of the God. I am separate from the bonds of nature, body, senses and mind. My natural shelter is my God. I do not become popper, poor, orphan or possessing a parent or guardian or a king with the increase and decrease of outside prosperity. I am always one essence. The changes which are taking place are the duties of the world, my soul has no duties. In this way think about the divinity of the soul and remove the negative thinking, because negative thinking makes a person sad, worried, and stressed. Negative thinking makes a person depressed and always immersed in the ocean of grief. Positive thinking person is always happy, normal, and cheerful even in the adverse situations. For this reason, the person should have positive thinking not only at the time of yoganidra or Shavasan but during the whole day. In this way we have thought positive about the divine form of the soul and gave rest to the mind and now we will think about the divine form of the God and give total rest to our soul.

Think that your soul has come out of the body and it is lying above the body in the sky and you are experiencing the with the internal soul that the body is lying on the ground just like a dead body. This is the reason that this asana is called Shavasan. Now devote your conscious strength to the God who is spread in the unending sky in the form of Supreme Soul Brahma. Think that your soul is getting the divine happiness of the God from all sides. Experience the divine happiness of the God's creation. The determination which is auspicious and with completed devotion towards God, is complete. You think of this God's nature and its divinity and concentrating on the wonderful form and creation of nature think of God's divinity. Think that you are in the valley of beautiful flowers, and the whole atmosphere is full of the scent of the different kinds of beautiful flowers. There is a kind of divinity on all sides. It is a great sight to see the God' creation. There is no end to God's creation. Along with the flower plants, there are beautiful fruits on the different trees, the God has filled each fruit with different flavors. A light breeze is flowing from all sides and giving immense happiness. In this beautiful garden the birds are chirping the divine songs of the God's creation. One can see God appearing from each flower, fruit. When we look at the sky it appears that the stars, the Moon and the Sun are like *diyas* in the huge universe in the form of temple. The rivers are flowing as if they are washing the feet of the God. Brahma is so great, unlimited, unbounded, unending. Oh God! Oh Father! Creator of the earth, Oh Mother! Take your son also in your shelter. Bless me with your divine happiness. Oh Lord! I should always get your divinity, calmness and enlightment. I should always remember your divine creation and immerse in you, and be engrossed in the unending happiness. Oh God! take me out of the worldly feelings and take me in the lap of happiness.

In this way take the incomparable happiness and once again experience yourself in the body. Imagine that you have returned back to the body after full sleep of Yoga. The respiration is on. Along with the breath the great power of life source is entering inside you. Experience yourself to be healthy, happy and cheerful and in the way the body was relaxed with determination in the same way and with the same determination experience the new power, consciousness and happiness in the body. Look at each organ from toe to the head and whichever organ you are seeing imagine that it is absolutely healthy. For example, if a person has pain in the knee or backache he should imagine that his pain has been relieved. By God's grace and practice of Yoga there is no pain in my knees and back, because Yoga cures the root cause of these diseases. The pain is coming out. In the same way there is any heart or stomach problem think that it has been cured. If there is any blockage in the arteries and the cholesterol level is high then think that the diseases are being cured. Take the vow that all the foreign particles, diseases, and deformities are going out and I am totally healthy. With these thoughts you should experience yourself to be physically and mentally healthy.

In the end experience that both the hands are totally powerful and healthy and rub both the palms against each other and keep the warm palms on your eyes and slowly open the eyes. This is the summarized method of Yoganidra and Shavasan. If anybody is unable to sleep then before going to bed, practice Shavasan and relax the body and feel tension free in the directed method and think of God's divinity and concentrate on the respiration and with every breath chant Omkar in the mind. While inhaling and exhaling meaningful chanting of Omkar should be done. The meaning of Omkar is - Brahma in the form of God, Omkar God is always in the form of truth, consciousness and cheerful. I am also getting happiness by praying the Omkar God. With these thoughts one should chant Omkar. The speed of inhaling and exhaling should be normal. In the same process count reverse from 100 to 1 and with each number chant Om. For example Om 10, Om 99, Om 98 etc. Praying in this way will put you off to deep sleep and you will get rid of bad dreams. In the daily yoga practice, this asana should be done after every difficult asana. After the end of practice, this asana should be done for 5 to 10 minutes.

Benefits:

1.   Mental stress, depression, high blood pressure, heart disease and insomnia are cured. These patients should do this asana regularly.

2.   Weakness of the nervous system, tiredness, negative thinking are cured.

3.   The body, mind, brain and soul gets total rest, power, zeal and happiness.

4.   The concentration power increases.

5.   Practicing Shavasan in between asanas relieves the tiredness of the body.

Makarasan (I)

Process

1.   Lie straight with your stomach towards the ground. While folding both the hands keep them on the opposite shoulders.

2.   Rest the forehead on the hands. There should be one foot distance between the legs.

3.   Relax the body like a dead body. While lying down in this position think of a dead body and concentrate yourself within the soul through wise thinking and

introspection. I am a separate life, pure-hearted and cheerful and flawless soul . This body is perishable. This body is the collection of five elements. When the time comes it merges in the same elements. This body and other riches remain here. We do not bring anything with us neither we will take anything along. In this way deviate your mind from the mortal world and experience the happiness of devotion to the Brahma present in the unending universe.

Makarasan (I)

Benefits :

1. This is the asana for rest. During rest a person feels light not only physically but also mentally. He is free from high blood pressure, mental tension and insomnia. In-between the asana this should be done for rest. The intestines of the stomach get natural massage which activates them and dysentery and other deformities are cured.

2. Since the hands are in passive stretching condition it affects the sympathetic nerves and helps in the relaxation of the body.

3. The heart does not function against the magnetic force, therefore it gets rest.

4. The internal secretion glands are benefited.

Balasan (Rest position)

Process:

1. Lie down with your stomach towards the ground keep the left hand under the head on the ground and turning the neck to the right keep the head on the hands, the left hand will be under the head and the left palm will be under the right hand.

2. Fold the right knee slightly, the way a child sleeps, lie down like that and rest. In the same way this asana is done from the other side.

Balasan (Rest Position)

Benefits:

Just like Shavasan, the tiredness of the body and mind is relieved.

Special asanas to reduce weight
Dwichakrikasan

Process :

1. Lie down straight towards your back and keep the hands below the hips, stop the breath, raise one leg fold up to the knee, bring the ankle near the hip and rotate in a cyclic motion. Repeat this from 10 to 30 times as per the capacity.

2. Similarly repeat the exercise with the second leg. Rotate the legs without touching the ground. Make a circular shape with the legs. Repeat this 10 to 30 times as per the capacity.

Dwichakrikasan (1)

3. When tired lie down in Shavasan and rest for some time and repeat the exercise in the opposite direction and rest when tired.

4. Repeat the exercise in next situation by rotating both the legs continuously in a circular motion. Inhale, fold one leg up to the knee and bring towards the chest, stretch the other leg straight up to the ground. Inhale and rotate the legs as if riding a bicycle. Then repeat this in the opposite direction continuously like a cycle. Those who do not have backache, heart disease or hernia can do the exercise with both the legs and then rest in Shavasan (see the picture below). Repeat this 5 to 10 times according to the capacity.

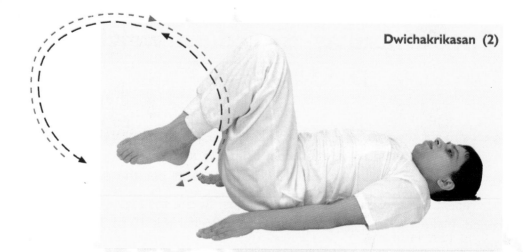

Dwichakrikasan (2)

Benefits:

1. This is the best exercise to reduce weight. If this is done regularly for 5 to 10 minutes, unnecessary weight can be reduced in minimum time.

2. It gives proper shape to the stomach. It activates the intestines. It cures constipation, dysentery, acidity etc.

3. In case of backache do the exercise by raising one leg, it is helpful for backache as well.

Padvritasan

Process

1. Lie down straight. Raise the right leg and make a circle by rotating the leg clockwise. In this way make 5 to 20 circles without touching the ground.

Padvritasan (1)

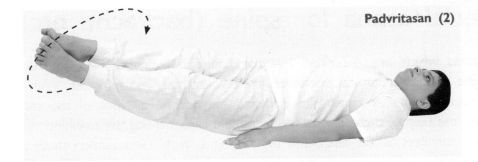

Padvritasan (2)

2. After rotating in one direction, rotate the leg in opposite direction (Anti-clockwise). when tired rest in Shavasan.

3. After doing this exercise with single leg do it with both the legs simultaneously. Rotate the legs up-down, right-left as much as you can. Rotate the legs clockwise and anti-clockwise directions.

Benefits:

1. This asana is also for reducing extra weight.

2. It definitely reduces the fat accumulated at hips, thighs and waist and gives proper shape to the stomach.

Ardhahalasan

Process:

This asana is like Uttanapadasan - the only difference is that in Uttanapadasan the legs are raised up to 30 degrees whereas in Ardhahalasan the legs are raised up to 90 degrees.

Ardhahalasan

Benefits:

All the benefits of Uttanapadasan are obtained with this asana. This asana is especially beneficial for reducing weight.

Special asana for spine (backache etc)

The asanas which are described here are specially beneficial to cure diseases related to the backache, cervical, sodalities, slip disc, sciatica, and spine etc. With God's grace we have completely cured slip disc and spinal cord diseases of thousands of patients with the help of these asanas. With the aim of benefiting the mankind with the scientific and harmless asanas instructed by the sages, with this intention these asanas are being instructed after practical experience. All these asanas are specially beneficial for the asthma patients, because the air is filled in lungs while doing all these exercises. This contracts and extends the lungs and the air is circulated there and the foreign particles are removed from there. The dead cells of the lungs reactivate. In this way these asanas are highly beneficial for the health of the lungs and cure respiratory problems. The stomach glands also become healthy with these asanas. Kidney problems are eliminated. In this way these asanas will cure a number of diseases and provide good health to the patients and the healthy person will not fall sick with the practice of these diseases.

Cautions:

The asanas which put lot of pressure on the stomach, those asanas should not be done by patients of ulcer, T.B of the intestine, hernia, liver and spleen enlargement.

Chakrasan

Process :

1. Lie down on your back and fold the knees. The ankle should be near the hips.

2. Take both the hands on the back side and keep them at the back of the shoulders at some distance, this will maintain the balance.

3. Inhale and lift the hips and chest upwards.

4. Slowly try to bring the hands and legs near, by which the body takes the shape of wheel.

5. While leaving the asana relax the body and rest the waist on the ground. Repeat this 3 to 4 times.

Benefits :

1. It makes the spinal cord flexible and stops ageing. It activates the stomach and the intestines.

2. It activates the body, gives energy, and increases the sharpness .

3. It is especially beneficial for hip pain, respiratory problem, eye problems, cervical and spondalitis.

4. It strengthens the muscles of hands and legs.

5. It cures the uterus problems in ladies.

Chakrasan

Setubandh Asan

Process:

1. Lie down straight.

2. Fold both the legs. Raise the hip area and raise both the hands with the support of the elbows and keep them under the waist.

3. Keeping the hip area above, straighten the legs. Rest the shoulders and the head on the ground. Remain in this position for 6 to 8 seconds.

Setubandh Asan

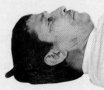

4. While coming back to normal position slowly rest the hips and legs on the ground. The hands should not be removed from the waist suddenly. Rest in Shavasan for some time and repeat the exercise 4 to 6 times.

Benefits:

This is beneficial in slip disc, backache, neck pain and stomach pain. Those who cannot do Chakrasan can get the benefits from this asana.

Markatasan (I)

Process:

1. Lie down straight and spread the hands at the shoulder level. The palms should open towards the sky. Then fold both the legs up to the knees and keep them near the hips.

2. Now turning the knees towards the right side, rest the right knee on the ground. Left knee should rest on the right knee and the left ankle should rest on the right ankle. Turn the neck to the left side.

3. Similarly repeat the exercise from left side as well.

Markatasan (I)

Benefits:

1. This exercise is especially useful for backache, cervical, spondalitis, slip disc, sciatica.

2. It cures stomach ache, dysentery, constipation, gas and makes the stomach light.

3. This is beneficial for the hip, joints pain. It cures all the deformities of the spine.

Markatasan (2)

Process:

1. Lie down in the above position. Fold both the legs and keep them near the hips. There should be a distance of one foot between the legs.

2. Now bending the left knee towards the right side rest it on the ground. Bend to an extent that the left knee should reach the right paw and rest the left knee on the right side on the right knee on the ground. Turn the neck to the left side.

3. Similarly repeat with the other leg.

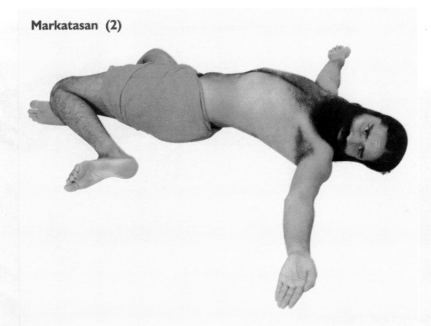

Markatasan (2)

Benefits:

As mentioned above. This is easier than the previous exercise.

Markatasan (3)

Process:

1. Lie down and spread both the hands in the level of the shoulders. The palms should be open towards the sky.

2. Raise the right leg 90 degrees and slowly take it near the left hand, turn the neck to the right side and stay in this position.

3. After this raise the leg straight upwards up to 90 degrees and slowly rest it on the ground.

4. Similarly repeat this exercise with the left leg.

5. In the end raise both the legs together up to 90 degrees and keep them near the hands. Turn the neck in the opposite direction and look to the right side and after some time straighten the legs.

6. In the same way raise both the legs and keep them near the hands on the right side. Turning the neck towards the left side and look at that side. This is one repetition in this way make 3 to 4 repetitions. Those who have severe pain in the neck they should not attempt with both the legs, they should do with single leg and do 2 to 3 repetitions.

Markatasan (3)

Benefits : As mentioned before.

Kati Uttanasan

Process:

1. Lie down in Shavasan and keep both the legs folded. Spread both the hands on the backside.

2. Inhale and raise the waist upwards. The hips and shoulders should rest on the ground. While exhaling bring down the back, press it and stretch it straight. Repeat this exercise 8 to 10 times.

Benefits: It is beneficial in slip disc, sciatica, and back pain.

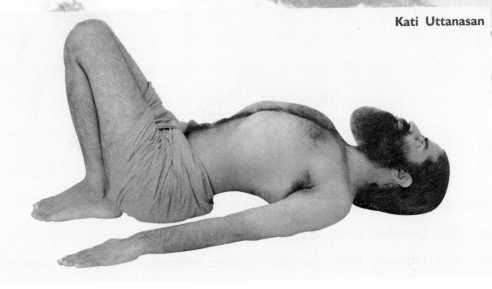

Kati Uttanasan

Makarasan (2)

Process:

1. Lie down straight on your stomach.

2. Join the elbows of both the hands and make a stand like thing, place the palms under the chin. Lift the chest up. Keep the elbows and legs together.

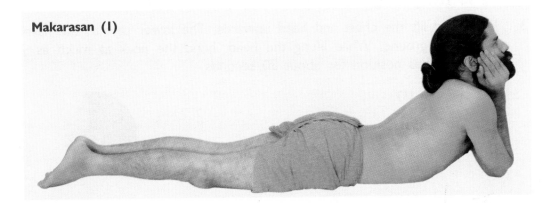

Makarasan (1)

3. Inhale and first fold one leg at a time and then both the legs. While folding the ankles should touch the hips. While exhaling unfold the legs. Repeat his 20 to 25 times.

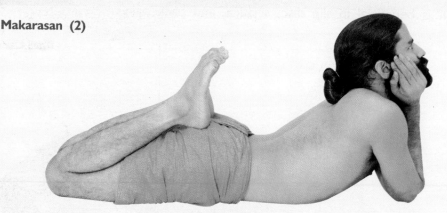

Makarasan (2)

Benefits:

1. It is beneficial in slip disc, cervical, and sciatica.

2. It is especially useful for asthma, lungs related problems, and knee pain.

Bhujangasan

Method:

1. Lie down on your stomach. Keep the alms on the ground and both the hands near both the sides of the chest. The elbows should be lifted up and the shoulders should be sticking to the body.

2. The legs should be straight and the paws should join together. The paws should be stretching straight backwards and resting on the floor.

3. Inhale and lift the chest and head upwards. The lower part of the navel should touch the ground. While lifting the head, bend the neck as much as you can, remain in this position for about 30 seconds.

Bhujangasan (1)

4. In this way repeat this exercise according to the capacity. After practicing this asana Bhujangasan and complete Bhujangasan can be done.

Bhujangasan (2)

Benefits:

It is important for cervical, spondalitis, slip disc, and all spine related problems.

Dhanurasan

Process

1. Lie down on your stomach. Fold the legs and keep the ankles on the hips. The knees and paws should be joined together.

2. Hold both the legs form the ankle portion with the hands.

3. Inhale and while lifting the knees and thighs stretch them upwards, hands should be straight. After lifting the lower portion, lift the stomach, chest, neck and head. The abdomen and navel area should rest on the ground. The shape of the body will be like the a bow. Remaining this position for about 10 to 30 seconds.

4. While exhaling come back to the original position. When the breathing is normal repeat this exercise. Do 3 to 4 repetitions.

Dhanurasan

Benefits:

1. It make the spine strong healthy and flexible. This asana is useful for cervical, spondalitis, backache, and stomach pain.

2. Shifting of the navel is avoided.

3. It is beneficial for the menstrual disorders related problems in females.

4. It cures the kidney and urinary problems It is beneficial in case of urination due to fear.

Purna Dhanurasan

Process

1. Lie down on your stomach. Fold both the legs from the back side and hold the toes with the hands.

2. While inhaling lift the hands, neck and head and from the back side both the legs from the ground, After remaining in this situation for some time, while exhaling rest the body parts on the ground.

Purna Dhanurasan

Benefits : As mentioned above

Shalabhasan (1)

Process :

1. Lie down with your stomach and place both the hands below the thighs.

2. Inhale and lift the right leg up, the leg should bend at the knee. The chin should rest on the ground. Remain in this position for 10 to 30 seconds. Do 5 to 7 repetitions.

Shalabhasan (1)

3. Similarly do with the left leg and then with the both legs for about 2 to 4 times.

Shalabhasan (1)

Benefits :

It cures all the diseases below the spine. It is especially beneficial for the backache, sciatica pain.

Shalabhasan (2)

Process :

1. Lie down on your stomach and touch the right hand with the head and the ear and lay them straight and keep the left hand on the waist at the back.

2. While inhaling lift the head, right hand and from the back lift the left leg above the ground level.

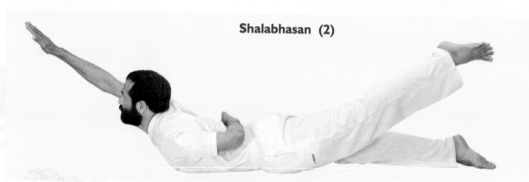

Shalabhasan (2)

3. Remain in this position for some time and slowly leave the asana. Similarly repeat this exercise from the left side.

Benefits:

It is beneficial for cervical, spondalitis, backache and other spinal problems.

Shalabhsan (3)

Process:

After the previous exercise take both the hand towards the back side and hold the wrist with each other hand. Inhale and lift the chest up as much as possible. Then slowly lift the body from both sides. While exhaling come back to the original position.

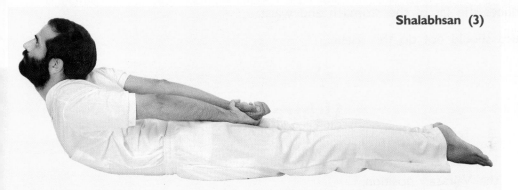

Shalabhsan (3)

Benefits : As mentioned above.

Vipreet Noukasan (Nabhi asan)

Process :

1. Lie down on your back and stretch both the hands in the front. The legs should join at the back and be straight. The paws should be stretched.

2. Inhale and lift the body from both sides. The legs, chest, head, and hands should be above the ground. Repeat this 4 to 8 times.

Vipreet Noukasan (Nabhi Asan)

Benefits:

1. It is beneficial for all the diseases of the spine.
2. It strengthens the navel area.
3. It releases gas.
4. It cures sex diseases and weakness.
5. It reduces the fat of the stomach and waist.
6. Females should not do this asana.

Ushtrasan

Process :

1. Sit in the Vajrasan position.
2. Now lift the ankles and keep both the hands on them. Keep the hands in such a manner that the fingers are towards inside and the big fingers are towards outside.

Ushtrasan

3. Inhale and bend the neck and head towards back and lift the waist. While exhaling sit down on the ankles. Repeat this 3 to 4 times.

Benefits :

1. This asana is good for respiratory system. The pores of the lungs strengthen and which benefits the patients of asthma.
3. It cures cervical, spondalitis, and sciatica and other spinal problems.
3. It is useful for thyroid.

Ardhachandrasan

Process :

1. Sit in Ushtrasan position and stand on the knees. Keep both the hands on the chest.

2. Inhale and bend the head and neck towards back side and lift the waist and stretch up.

3. When the head is bend backwards and rests on the ankles it is called purna Chankrasan

Benefits:

The benefits of this asana are same as Ushtrasan. Those who cannot do Ushtrasan they can benefit from this asana.

Ardhachandrasan

Trikonasan

Process:

1. Keeping a distance of one foot between the legs stand straight. Both the hands should be spread towards the shoulders.

2. Inhale and bringing the left hand from the front and rest it on the left paw on the ground, otherwise keep the hand near the ankle and lift the right hand upwards and bend the neck to the right side and look at the right hand. Then while exhaling come back to the original position and repeat the exercise from the other side.

Trikonasan

Benefits :

The hip area becomes flexible. The fat on the sides is reduces. With the pressure on the back side the muscles become healthy. The chest expands.

Surya Namaskar

Surya namaskar gives complete health, strength and energy to the body and activates all the body parts. The internal glands and the secretion, hormones processes of the body is balanced. If possible do this exercise at the time of sunrise. According to capacity 11 to 21 repetitions can be done.

Process :

1.   Stand facing towards the Sun, fold the hands in the position of namaskar and keep on the chest.

Surya Namaskar (1)

Surya Namaskar (1 & 12)

Surya Namaskar (2 & 11)

2.   Inhale, stretch the hands in the front and take them back. Look towards the sky. bend the waist towards backside as much as possible.

3.   Exhale and bend the hands towards front and rest them near the legs on the ground. If possible touch the ground with the palms and try to touch the knees with the head.

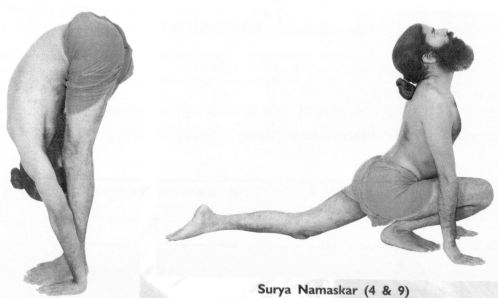

Surya Namaskar (3 & 10)

Surya Namaskar (4 & 9)
Right foot forward in method no. 4
Left foot forward in method no. 9

4.   Now bend forwards place the hands on both sides of the chest. Lift the left leg and take it back as done in Bhujangasan. Let the right leg be in between both the hands. Knee should be in front of the chest and rest the ankle on the ground. Look towards the sky and stop the breath inside.

Surya Namaskar (5 & 8)

Surya Namaskar (6)

5. Inhale and take the right leg back. The neck and head should be in between the hands. Lift the hips and waist and bend down the head and look at the navel.

6. Keeping the hands, legs and paws straight, touch the knees and chest on the ground. In this way, when two hands, two legs, two knees, chest and head touch the ground it becomes Sashtangasan. Keep the breathing normal.

Surya Namaskar (7)

7. Inhale and lift the chest up and look at the sky, rest the waist on the ground, and keep the legs and hands straight.

8. As mentioned in step 5.

9. As mentioned in step 4. Change the position of the legs. In this case keep the left leg in between both the hands.

10. As mentioned step 3.

11. As mentioned in step 2.

12. As mentioned in step 1.

Benefits :

1. Surya namaskar is a complete exercise. With this all the body parts and joints become strong and healthy.

2. It makes the stomach, intestines, pancreas, heart and lungs totally healthy.

3. It makes the spinal cord and waist flexible and cures their deformities.

4. It regulates the blood circulation in the entire body and in this way cures the blood impurities and destroys the skin disease.

5. The muscles of hands, legs, shoulders, thighs, become strong and toned up.

6. It increases mental strength, sharpness and vitality of the brain.

7. It is also useful for diabetes.

8. Surya namskar gives complete health to the body.

Miscellaneous Asanas

Shirshasan

Process :

1. Make a cushion out of a long cloth or dhoti. Interlock the fingers of both the hands and rest the hands till elbows on the ground. Keep the cushion in between the cushion.

2. The front portion of the head should rest on the cushion and knees should rest on the ground. now controlling the body weight on the neck and elbows lift the legs straight in the level of the ground.

3. Now while bending one knee lift it straight after this lift the second leg and bend up to the knee.

4. Now one by one try to lift the legs, do not hurry in the beginning. Slowly the legs will be straight. When the legs are straight, then in the beginning join them and bend them slightly forward otherwise there is a chance to fall back.

Shirshasan

5.   Eyes should be closed, the breathing should be normal.

6.   The steps which were followed to lift the legs follow the same steps to come back to the original position. According to your constitution do Shavasan or stand up straight after Shirshasan. So that the blood circulation which was towards the brain becomes normal.

Time : In the beginning do this exercise for 15 seconds and slowly take it to 30 minutes. Incase you wish to practice it for a longer time you should do it under the supervision of an expert. In normal conditions it is sufficient to do it for 5 to10 minutes.

Benefits:

1.   This asansa is the king of all exercises. This provides pure blood to the brain, which makes the ears, nose and other organs healthy. It makes the pituitary and pineal glands healthy and activates the brain. It increases memory, sharpness and concentration.

2.   It activates the digestive system, stomach, intestines, and liver and increases the fire of the stomach, enlargement of the intestines, swelling of the intestines, hysteria, hydrosol, hernia, constipation, varicose veins, and other diseases are cured.

4.   It activates the thyroid glands and reduces both obesity and weakness, because both these diseases are due to the irregularity in the thyroid function.

4.   It activates thyroid gland and stabilises the celibacy. It cures bad dreams, disease in which the vital humors of the body are secreted through urine, impotency and infertility. It increases the shine and vigor on the face.

5.   Untimely falling of hair, graying of the hair and other diseases are cured.

Cautions :

1.   Those who have pain in the ears or there is secretion form ears and they should not do this asana.

2.   If there is long-sightedness or if the eyes are red, do not do it.

3.   Patients of heart, high blood pressure and back pain should not do this.

4.   Do not do Shirshasan after doing heavy exercises. The body temperature should be normal while doing this asana.

5.   Do not do this exercise while cold and cough.

Ekpada - Grivasan

Process :

Sit in Dandasan and fold the left leg from the knee and keep it in front of the groin. Then lift the right leg from the back side and fix it on the neck. Now keep both the hands in front in namaskar position. Remain in this position for one and half to two minutes. Then come back to the original position and repeat the exercise with the other leg.

Benefits:

1. The shoulders and chest become strong with this exercise.

2. The parts of the leg become flexible and strong. The leg muscles become strong.

3. Many stomach problems are cured. Fat reduces.

Grivasan

Sidhasan

Process:

1. Sit in Dandasan and fold the left leg and place the ankle in between the genital and rectum. The ankle of the right leg should be kept on the upper portion of the genital. The ankle bone of the left leg should be above the ankle bone of the right leg. The paws should in between the thighs and the calf of the leg.

2. The knees should rest on the ground. Both the hands should be Gyan mudra (touch the index finger and the big finger, remaining three fingers should be

straight) and resting on the knees. The spine should be straight. Eyes closed and concentrate the mind in between the eyebrows.

Sidhasan

Benefits:

1. It has been practiced by learned persons therefore it is called Sidhasan. It protects celibacy and makes a person celibate.

2. It cools down the lust for sex and removes the inattentiveness of the mind. This is the best asana for awakening the kundilini.

3. It is beneficial for piles and sex diseases.

Yog Sadhna
&
Yoga Healing Secrets

Kukkutasan

Kukkutasan

Process :

1. Sit in Padmasan, put the hands in between the thighs and the calf muscles and rest them on the ground.

2. Inhale and put the pressure on the palms lift the elbows and the body above the ground. When tired slowly come down.

Benefits : The nerves of hands and shoulders become strong.

Uttan Kukkutasan

Uttan Kukkutasan

Process :

1. Sit in Padmasan and keep the hands in the front.

2. Place the knees firmly on the elbows and the shoulders below the chest, inhale and lift the body by putting the body weight on the hands.

Benefits : as mentioned above.

Supta Garbhasan

Process:

1. Sit in Padmasan and lie down on your back. Like kukkutasan take out the hands from in between the thighs and calf muscles.

Supta Garbhasan

2. Tie the hands at the back. Keep the breathing normal. This can be done by holding the neck or ears with the hands.

Benefits : It is useful for hands, legs, waist and stomach.

Garbhasan

Process : Sit in Padmasan, take out the hands from in-between the thighs and the calf and hold the ears. The weight of body will be on the hips.

Benefits : It increases the fire of the stomach. It is useful for the complete digestive system.

Garbhasan

Tolangulasan

Tolangulasan

Process :

Sit in Dandasan, balancing the body weight on the hands, inhale and lift the body, legs along with the hips above the ground.

Benefits:

It gives good strength to the nerves of hands and legs.

Mayurasan

Process :

1   Join both the hands in the front and turn the fingers towards backside, first sit on the knees.

2.   Inhale and place the elbows on both sides of the navel slowly straighten the legs towards back. The whole body weight will be on the elbows. In the completion stage the head and legs will be above the ground at equal levels.

Mayurasan

Benefits :

1.   It benefits spleen, liver, kidneys, pancreas and stomach. It brings shine on the face.

2.   It is beneficial for the patients of diabetes. It cures constipation.

3.   It increases the fire of the stomach.

Parvatasan

Parvatasan

Process :

1. Sit in Padmasan and stand up straight with the support of knees.

2. Keep both the hands above the head in the namaskar position.

Benefits : It increases the concentration of the mind.

Utkatasan

Process :

Utkatasan

The paws should be resting on the ground and the ankles on the hips. Keep both the hands on the knees and spread the knees in equal level of the ankles.

Benefits : It is useful for celibacy, it cures piles.

Yog Sadhna
&
Yoga Healing Secrets

Sinhasan

Process :

1. If possible face towards the Sun, sit in Vajrasan and spread the knees. The fingers of the hands should be turning backside and keep them straight in between the legs.

2. Inhale and take out the tongue. Look in between the eyebrows and exhale. While exhaling roar like a lion. Repeat his 3 to 4 times.

3. After doing Sinhasan leave the saliva from the mouth and lightly massage the throat, this prevents soar throat.

Sinhasan

Benefits :

1. It is useful for tonsils, thyroid and other throat problems.

2. It is beneficial in ear-problems and unclear pronunciation.

3. It is beneficial for the children who lisp(speak indistinctly)

Yog Sadhna
&
Yoga Healing Secrets

Marjarasan

Process :

1. Take the position by resting both the palms and knees on the ground.

Marjarasan (1)

2. Now inhale and lift the head and the chest, bend the waist downwards. Remain in this position for sometime, exhale and lift the back and bend the head down. Repeat this 5 to 6 times.

Marjarasan (2)

Benefits :

1. It is useful in hip pain and rashes in the rectum. It strengthens the lungs.

2. It cures the disease in which the uterus moves out.

Vrischikasan

Process :

1. Sit and keeping a distance between the hands and rest the elbows on the ground.

2. Now like Shirshasan rest the head in between the hands and lift the legs. When the legs go up try to lift the head. In the beginning some difficulty will be experienced. When practiced a scorpion like shape appears with the head and legs. In the completion stage try to keep the legs over the head.

Vrischikasan

Vrischikasan
(Final position)

Benefits:

1. It increases the fire of the stomach and cures all the stomach problems.

2. It cures urinary problems and brings shine on the face.

Prasruthasta vrischikasan

Process:

Lie down on your stomach, bring up both the legs with strength , fold then and keep it on the head. This asana is very difficult and therefore there may be some problems in the beginning.

Benefits : as mentioned above.

Prasruthasta Vrischikasan

Padangushtasan

Process :

1. Keep the right ankle in between the genitals and the rectum.

2. Keep the left leg above the right thigh. Now rest both the hands on both sides balance the body on the ankles and paws and lift the hands make the namaskar position. Try and remain in this position for some time. Keep the breathing normal.

3. After doing with one leg repeat the asana with other leg.

Benefits :

It is useful for celibacy. When practiced for long time, kundilini awakes and the sperm rises above. It increases the strength, intelligence and vigour.

Padangushtasan

Yog Sadhna
&
Yoga Healing Secrets

Brahmacharyasan

Process :

1. Sit in Vajrasan and fold the paws towards outside with the help of the hands. The ankles should be towards inside near the hips and the paws should be outside.

2. Both the knees should be together, keep the hands on the knees. The back should be straight and breathing should be normal. As per capacity do it for 5 to 30 minutes.

Benefits :

This asana is beneficial for celibates and as the name suggest the qualities are also the same. It cures all kinds of humor related problems, bad dreams, disease in which the vital humors of the body are secreted through urine, diabetes, etc.

Brahmacharyasan

Gorakshasan

Process :

1. Keep both the ankles joint together in the front.

2. Now place the middle portion between the groins and rectum on the ankles and sit down. Both the knees should rest on the ground. Keep the hands in Gyamudra on the knees.

Benefits :

1. It is the completing exercise for Brahmacharyasan. After practicing the previous asana, do this asana with the

Gorakshasan

Yog Sadhna
&
Yoga Healing Secrets

position of the legs in the opposite direction, which regulates the blood circulation in the muscles and makes them healthy.

2. Since in this asana *moolbandh* is done naturally, it is useful for celibates. It stops the wavering of the senses and calms down the mind. that is why it is called Gorakshasan.

Akarnadhanushtaamkarasan

Process:

1. Sit in Dandasan. Fold the right leg and keep it on the left leg.

2. Hold the big toe of the right leg with left hand and big toe of the left leg with right hand.

3. Inhale and bring the right leg to the left ear. Remain in this position for some time. Again come back in the Dandasan position. In the same way do with the other leg.

Akarnadhanushtaamkarasan

Benefits :

1. It relieves the hands and legs pain and strengthens their glands.

2. This is beneficial in vertigo.

Bhunamanasan

Process :

1.   Sit in Dandasan and spread the legs on both the sides as much as you can.

2.   Hold the toes with both the hands, while exhaling touch the ground with the chest and stomach.

     The chin also should touch the ground. Remain in this position for some time.

Bhunamanasan

Benefits : It cures thighs, legs, waist, stomach and back problems and stabilises the sperm.

Skandhpadasan

Process:

1.   Sit in Dandasan, lift the left leg with the help of hands and keep it on the neck.

2.   Keep the hands in front of the chest in namsakar pose. Keep the waist and head straight.

3.   Similarly do with the other leg.

Benefits:

It provides strength to the nerves of hands, legs, and neck.

Skandhpadasan

Yog Sadhna
&
Yoga Healing Secrets

Dwipadagrivasan

Dwipadagrivasan

Process:

1. Sit in Dandasan and keep the legs one by one on the neck.
2. Balancing the body weight on the hips, keep the hands in namaskar position. Try to remain in this position for some time.

Benefits : Same as Skandhapadasan.

Bakasan

Process :

1. Firmly rest the palms on the ground and rest the knees over the elbows on the hands..

2. Inhale balancing the weight slowly try to lift the legs above the ground. When practiced the position will be like crane.

Benefits: It strengthens the nerves of the hands and gives them good health. It increases the shine of the face.

Bakasan

Yog Sadhna
&
Yoga Healing Secrets

Updhanasan (takiyasan)

Process :

1. Sit in Dandasan, fold the left leg and place it on the neck with the help of the hands.

2. Rest the right elbow on the ground and keep the hand on the head and lie down on the ground.

3. The right leg should lie straight on the ground. keep the left hand straight and keep it on the left thigh.

4. In the same way change the leg and do the asana.

Updhanasan (Takiyasan)

Benefits : It strengthens the nerves of the hands, legs and neck.

Hatapadangushtasan

Hatapadangushtasan

Process :

1. Stand straight, lift the left leg and keep it on the right thigh and hold the big toe of the left leg with the right hand.

2. Keep the left hand on the hips. The big finger of the hand should be towards the back and fingers towards the stomach.

3. Balancing the body weight on the right leg, stretch the left leg in the front (holding the big toe with the right hand). While you hold the leg, the hand also become straight. After doing this with one leg do it with the other leg.

Benefits : It cures the diseases of the legs and hands. It is the best exercise for people suffering with vertigo.

Yog Sadhna
&
Yoga Healing Secrets

Dhruvasan

Process:

1. Stand straight and lift the right leg and keep it on the left thigh in such a way that the paw and ankle should be near the beginning of the thigh and paw facing down.

2. Make the namaskar pose with both the hands. Remain in this position for as long as you can and repeat the exercise with the other leg.

Benefits: It removes the wavering of the mind. It develops the nervous system and makes it stable.

]

Konasan

Process :

1 Stretch the legs with a distance of one and half foot between them and stand straight.

Konasan

2. Inhale and touch the left paw with the right hand and bend the left hand up and bend towards right side as much as possible. The ankles and paws should rest on the ground. The body should be bend only from the sides. One should not bend forward or backward. Remain in this position for 4 to 6 seconds and repeat this 4 to 6 times.

3. Similarly change the hand touch the right paw with the left hand.

Benefits: It is especially useful in curing the weakness of waist, ribs and lungs. It is useful for the women as well. It reduces the fat from the waist and gives good shape to the waist.

Garudasan

Garudasan

Process :

Stand straight, turn the right leg from the front and fold it on the left leg. Fold both the hands in the same way and come in the namaskar pose. After doing from one side repeat it from the other side.

Benefits :

1. This is beneficial for hydrosol, male's genital glands and kidney.

2. It cures the pain in the hands-legs and any other deformity.

3. It cures the urinary problems.

Vrikshasan

Process:

1. Stand straight and rest both the hands on the ground, keep a distance of 6 inches between the hands.

2. Taking the body weight in the hands slowly raise the legs above the ground and stabilize them straight like a tree.

Benefits:

1. It increases strength, shine and sperm in the body.

2. It cures eye disorders, humor related problems and phlegm problems. It makes the hands beautiful and shapely.

3. It regulates blood circulation in the heart and lungs and makes them healthy.

Vrikashasan

Tadasan

Tadasan

Process:

Stand in the previous position and take both the hands on the sides and while taking deep breath raise the hands. As the hands are raised simultaneously the ankles should also be raised. The body weight will be on the paws and the body will be stretched up fully.

Benefits:

1. Due to deep breath the lungs get strength.

2. It is good to increase the height. This develops the nerves of the body and activates them.

Pakshyasan

Pakshyasan

Process:

1. Stand straight and place the left leg on the neck and shoulder.

2. Stretch the hands on both sides. The right leg should be absolutely straight. Keep the hands in namaskar pose.

3. After doing it with left leg repeat thee exercise with right leg.

Benefits : This asana brings activity and makes the body light. It develops the nerves of the thighs. It cures the brain related problems.

Padahastasan

Padahastasan

Process :

Stand straight and while inhaling raise the hands and bend forwards. Touch the knees with the head. The hands will be at the back near the ankle bone.

Benefits: It makes the waist and stomach healthy. It is beneficial for increasing the height.

Natarajasan

Natarajasan

Process :

1. Stand straight and turn the right leg towards the back. Take the right hand from above the shoulder and hold the big toe of the right leg.

2. The left hand will be raised straight up. After doing it with one leg repeat with the next leg.

Benefits: It develops the nerves of the hands and legs. It strengthens the nervous system.

Vatayanasan

Process :

1. Stand in the previous position and fold the left leg and place it at the beginning of the right thigh in such a manner that the paw is on the thigh and the ankle is that beginning of the groin.

2. Folding the right leg, rest the left knee on the ground. The hands should be in namaskar pose. in the same way do it with the other hand.

Benefits : It is beneficial in the knee problems. The body becomes light. It increases the water quantity in the thighs. It is beneficial for patients of hernia.

Vatayanasan

Hathyoga and Shatkarma

Lord Shiva is considered to be the creator of hathyoga. Under his tradition Shri Matsyendrnath, Swami Gorakshnath, Meenanath, Chouranginath, Swatmaram and others up to Bhartruhari and Gopichand have kept the tradition alive. With hathyoga we can make our body pure, healthy and clean and obtain kingship, in the way the illuminator of hathyoga says:

"kevalam rajayogam...." this means hathyoga is advised only to enter into the kingship, because kingship includes purification of the internal self through resistance to wards passions and following the rules and to enter meditation and deep meditation. However, if we are unhealthy, if our conscious is dead then it is impossible to obtain the state of deep meditation. Therefore hathyoga pradipika further says that:

केवलं राजयोगाय हठविद्योपदिश्यते

(Hathyoga-2/76)

This means kingship cannot be obtained without austerity and kingship is incomplete without austerity. There fore the devotee should thoroughly practice both austerity and kingship in balanced manner. Normally people think that hathyoga means the yoga which is done by capturing the power, however this meaning is totally opposite. The classics define hathyoga(austerity) as:

हठं बिना राजयोगं राजयोगं बिना हठं ।
न सिध्यति ततो युग्मानिष्पत्ते सम यसत्॥

Hakar represents right nostril and thakar represents left nostril. The combination of left and right nostril accomplishes hathyoga. The left nostril is known as chandra nadi and right nostril is known as surya nadi. They both are present in our body. We get the power of life with these two only. Here it is sufficient to write that a person has two types of powers- one is power of the fire - strength, courage, braveness, boldness and the second is power of the nectar - respect, calmness, patience, harmony, love and sympathy. A person's behavior is fulfilled with these. Vombining power of fire and power of nectar and creating a divine power is a yogic action. There is a science related to (surya) right nostril and (soma) left nostril which is known as nerve science or swara science, which has been described in brief.

Nerve or Science of Voice

''यथा ब्रह्माण्डे तथा पिण्डे'' according to this all the powers of outside world are within us. We need not obtain power form outside, we need to recognise the powers within us and to utilise them properly in a balanced way. The basis of outside world are the Sun and the Moon. These two administer the world. These are representatives of power of the fire and power of the nectar. In the same way there are Sun and

Moon voices within us. Voice of the moon represents nectar. This develops piousness, modesty, power, happiness and will power in the person. The voice of the Sun is full of strength, courage, boldness and the ability to fulfill the desires. With the balance between these two powers a third power is created, which is established in between these two powers, this is called the ray of the Sun. These voices in hathyoga are known by the names of Ganga, Yamuna, and Saraswati.

इण भगवती गंगा, पिंगला यमुना नदी।
इडा पिंगलयोर्मध्ये बालरंडा च कुंडली।।

(Hathyoga - 3/110)

Ida means the right nostril which is Goddess Ganga. Pingala is the left nostril, which is goddess Yamuna. in between these lies the center nerve, which is the ray of the Sun. which is also called Saraswati or kundali. Saint Kabirdas says :

चाँद सूरज तो बने मसालची, सूरत सुहागनी नाच रही।
इडा पिंगला ताना भरनी, सुखमन तार से बीनी चदरिया।
घट में गंगा, घट में यमुना, घ्ट में ठाकुरद्वारा।।

Which Means,

Now we shall throw some light on the Shatkarma included in Hathyoga Shatkarma, means the six actions enjoined on a brahman. The sages gave the education of shatkarma to their disciples for the purification of the body and obtaining kingship. These actions rejuvenate the human body and makes them disease free, with longevity, health, strength, and full of vigour. Shatkarma षटकर्म निर्गत स्थौल्य कफदोषमवाधिक। प्राणायामं तत कुर्यादनायासेन सिध्यति।

Which means, the actions of the shatkarma purify a corpulence body and they are equally important in the purification of lean bodies. By practicing these actions 20 types of different diseases like phlegm, wind related problems, bile problems, leprosy, stomach problems, lungs disorder, heart and liver problems are cured. Therefore for the benefit of the mankind these actions are being described here.

(Hathyoga 2/22)

धौतिर्बस्तिस्तथा नेतिस्त्राटकं नौलिकं तथा कपालभातिश्चैतानि षट् कर्माणि प्रचक्षते।

धौतिर्ब्हस्तिस्तथा तेति नौलिकी स्त्राटकस्तथा।
कपालभाति षट्कर्माणि सम यसेत्

(Goraskhasamhita)

Dhouti (washing), basti (sucking water or air through rectum), neti (accepting through nose), tratak(staring), nouli(rotating the stomach) and kapalbhati (type of pranayam), these six actions have been advised by the profounder of Yoga. A yoga ambitious person should practice them strictly. Their description is being made here.

1. Neti : Accepting different types of fluids through nose is called neti.

Types of Neti:

a) Jal neti b) Sutra neti c) Ghrutneti d) Dugdh neti i.e., water, thread, ghee and milk respectively.

Jalneti

a) **Jalneti :** Add 10 gms of rock salt in one litre of lukewarm water and pour it in the neti container. The morning time is best for neti. Incase of particular disease it can be done twice a day. Put the pipe of the container in the right nostril and keep the left nostril slightly below. Open the mouth slightly and breath through mouth. The water will start coming out from the left nostril on its own. Similarly do it with the other nostril. If there is no phlegm, neti can be performed without salt in cold water. Those who have cough and cold should do it with lukewarm salted water only. Those who do not have phlegm they should start with warm water and slowly do with normal water. Neti cures cold and running nose but some people catch cold by doing neti. After neti kapalbhati should also be done so that the water stuck up in the pipes comes out and the person does not catch cold.

Sutraneti

b) Sutra neti (thread) : Sutra neti is done with a thread made out of cotton. The thread should be put in water before putting it in the nose. After soaking in water it should be slightly bent at the corners, so that it can easily enter the nose. Now slowly put the thread in the left nostril, when it comes into the mouth take it out with the help of hands.

Note : In case thread is not available, no: 4 and 5 catheter can be used for the purpose. Sutraneti creates a light pain in the nose and in throat, therefore after this ghrutneti or telneti should be done.

c) Ghrut neti (ghee) : Sit on a chair or lie down on bed and keep the head towards backside. With the help of dropper pour 8 to 10 drops of pure luke warm ghee in the nostrils. In the same way oil neti is also done. Drinking milk from nostrils is called dugdh neti. After practicing the jal neti perfectly dugdh neti should be done. In dugdh neti the milk is not allowed to fall from the nostril as in case of jal neti, instead the milk is slowly swallowed inside.

Benefits : In *Hathyoga Pradipika* neti is said to purify the forehead, increase the eyesight, curing the all the diseases of the throat.

कपाल शोधनी चैव दिव्य दृष्टि प्रदायनी।
जत्रध्वर्वजातरोगौघं नेतिराशु निहन्ति च।।

Neti definitely cures the cold, running nose and phlegm related problems. It is extremely beneficial in eye problem, graying of hair, headache and other diseases. The purpose of neti is not only cleansing the nose but also protecting the phlegmatic tissue from external pollution, dust particles, smoke, heat, cold, bacteria and other germs and make it capable. Some people have very sensitive phlegmatic tissue, which gets afflicted by external atmosphere, this is called allergy,. Neti reduces the sensitivity of phlegmatic tissue and cures all the problems. In some people the bone in the nose increases. In this situation sinuses can be cured with neti in the beginning stage itself.

2. Dhouti(Washing):

Dhouti is done for cleaning the stomach. Dhouti means to wash. It has four classifications - Vaman dhouti, gajkarani, vastradhouti, danda dhouti.

a) Vaman dhouti: (vomiting)

Procedure: This action should be after getting free from the morning chores. For this activity, prepare I to 2 litres of lukewarm water with salt try to drink as much as possible,. bend 10 degrees forward, put the two middle fingers in the throat, this will cause vomiting and the water will come out. In this way with the touch of the fingers the whole water will come out. Those who have red eyes should not do this action forcibly. One should not bend forward too much and the legs should be kept close to each other. This action is also known as badhi .

Benefits: The phlegm in the stomach, bile and undigested food etc. comes out with vamna dhouti. Those who have phlegm disease, respiratory problem, asthma and acidity should do this action. Afterwards when the disease starts curing, reduce the action also. Dhouti removes acidic bile and fever reduces with perspiration. This also stops the dizziness and other problems. This action should normally done once a week.

Vaman Dhouti (I)   Vaman Dhouti (2)

b) Gajkarani or Kunjar action:

The only difference between vaman dhouti and gajakarani is that in the first case the water comes out in gaps, whereas in gajakarani the whole water comes out at a time. Gaja or kunjar means elephant. As an elephant fills water in its trunk and throws it all at a time like a fountain in the same way this action takes place therefore it is called gajakarani, means doing like the elephant.

Process : Drink as much water as you can, drink water and bend the waist 10 degrees forward. Contract the throat, mouth and neck like Ujjayi and inhale as we do while drinking water, take gulps in the same way and push the air in the stomach. contract the stomach. This will contract the abdomen and the whole water will come out like a fountain. In this you can put slight pressure on the abdomen with the left hand.

Benefits : As mentioned before.

c) Vastra dhouti (cloth)

Procedure: Take a muslin cloth 22 feet in length and width which is equal to four fingers (around 2 inches). Fold in a circle and leave it a vessel containing boiled water for 4 to 5 minutes. Sit on your feet and keep the edge of the cloth on the front portion of the tongue. Now slowly swallow the cloth along with the saliva as we do in the case of food. In the middle, drink little water as well, this will help in swallowing the cloth easily. In the beginning vomiting sensation will occur. If vomiting comes close your mouth. In the beginning 3 to 4 feet of cloth will go inside. With practice you will be able to swallow the whole cloth. After swallowing the cloth stand up and do *uddiyan bandh* and *nouli*. After doing nouli action sit down and take out the cloth. If the cloth gets stuck in between then swallow a little and then take it out. Take it out and wash it with detergent and keep it safe.

Vastra Dhouti (1)   **Vastra Dhouti (2)**

Cautions:

1. While swallowing the cloth you should not press it with the teeth.

2. While swallowing the cloth at least one foot should be left outside.

3. After swallowing the cloth it is necessary to take it out after 20 minutes otherwise the last edge of the cloth can reach the abdomen and get digested, which can be harmful. Therefore after 15 to 20 minutes whatever length of cloth has been swallowed, it should be taken out.

4. Those who get acidic belches or have any type of ulcer in the stomach, they should not do this action.

Benefits :

1. Vastradhouti removes the phlegm covering collected on the membrane of the stomach, with which the digestive juice produces and appetite increases.

2. It is especially beneficial for phlegm patients. This action is important in stomach pain due to indigestion.

d) Dand Dhouti

Process : Boil 3 feet long and 6 mm. wide soft rubber tube in water, so that it is disinfected. the edge which is to be put inside the mouth should be first rubbed on a stone. Drink lukewarm water added with salt at least 1 to 2 glasses. Now bend forward and stand. Put one edge of the pipe in the mouth and try to swallowing it. Swallow the pipe to the extent that its other edge reaches the stomach. The other edge will hanging outside. As soon as the pipe reaches the stomach the water starts coming out due to sifan action. In this, take out the whole water.

Caution : Before using the pipe it should be stretched and checked. Other wise there a chance of breaking and remaining in the stomach.

enefits : When the faecal matter accumulates on the fluid secretion glands of the gestive system in the stomach, then the digestive juice is produced in very little antity. In this action the walls of the wind pipe become excited and get relaxed due reverse action, due to which the phlegm comes out. In asthma the wind pipe gets ntracted, which is removed with this action, which stops the asthma attacks.

Rejuvenation actions - Shankh dhouti (Conch shell) or purification of the Intestine

The shape of our intestine is like a conch shell. Purification of the conch shell aped intestine is called shank purification or varisar action. We have experienced this tion on several patients and found that this really rejuvenates the person. This ocess is useful in curing serious indigestion problems. There is no disease in which is action is not effective like all kinds of stomach problems, obesity, piles, high blood essure, diabetes, humor related problems. We have found in yoga camps to the tent that half of the benefits are due to the yoga asanas and actions and rest half are te to this process. We clean our clothes everyday. If we do not wash our clothes en for one day they get dirty. Our stomach contains around 32 feet long intestine, e never clean it in our lives. This results in accumulation of light dirt layer on its walls. ue to this dirty layer, the excretion and secretion of juices does not take place operly, which causes dysentery, indigestion, acidic belches, and other diseases. When e faecal matter gets decomposed the stomach starts stinking. It causes gastric buble. The juice is not produced properly. When the main organ becomes deformed en the subsidiary organs like abdomen, pancreas etc are also affected and cause fferent types of diseases.

Our body is an instrument. Out of the seven wonders of the world, the biggest onder is that who created this wonderful instrument? As we do overhauling of the usical instruments, motor car, watch etc. so that these machines function properly, the same way we should do the servicing and overhauling of our body which is in e form of instrument so that it remains healthy, with longevity and strong.

equired items for this process:

One glass of water (to drink), lukewarm water which contains proportionate nount of lime juice and rock salt, kichdi made out of rice and moong dal, 100 gms pure ghee per head made out of cow milk Incase ghee made out of cow milk is ot available you can use buffalo milk, mat or blanket for doing the asana, light bed eet to cover, and a toilet near the bed.

Prior preparation: before beginning the purification of the intestine practice asana should start one week before the day on which this process is to be done. O the day before light meals should be taken at around 8 in the night. In the eveni drink 50 to 100 gms. of milk with raisins, this will facilitate the purification process. C to bed before 10 pm. On the next day get up in the morning and get free for bath, excretion, brushing the teeth etc. Incase the excretion does not happen it do not mater.

Three types of water:

1. **Lime and rock salt water :** Add lime juice and rock salt in the water normal quantity and make it warm. All healthy persons except patients of hi blood pressure, phlegm and wind related problems can drink this water.

2. **For the patients of wind and phlegm related diseases:** Incase joints pain, gout, swelling, cervical, spondalitis, slipdisc, and any other type physical pain and phlegm related problems should take warm water added wi rock salt.

3. **For the patients of high blood pressure and skin diseases:** Peop who have high blood pressure and skin disease should drink hot water added with lim juice and then do this process.

Process : Sit in Utkatasan (on your feet) and drink one or two glasses of prepare water as directed. Then do two repetitions of the five asanas prescribed for purificatic of the intestine and drink water as per desire. After drinking water repeat th exercises. In this way repeating the exercises and drinking water in between will resu in bowels. Do not try hard to pass the bowels. Pass the bowels in the quantity as comes. While sitting in the toilet, do ashwini action (contracting and expanding th rectum), this will clean the stomach and piles and other diseases will also cure. Aft coming out of the toilet drink water and do the exercises. In this way drink water, c the exercises and pass the bowels. When you go the toilet 8 to 10 times he you w see that yellow water stops coming. The water which you are drinking the same wate is coming out of the rectum. Then drink 4 to 5 glasses of water as desired and c vaman dhouti. After 30 to 40 minutes of doing vaman dhouti lie down in Shavasan ar rest. Cover the body with light cloth, because the body should not get exposed t wind. After 30 to 40 minutes prepare light kichdi with rice and moong dal add require quantity of ghee and consume it. This action purifies the entire body.

 122

ter purification the body should be greased in the same way as it is done for
hicles. After this action, the ghee which is consumed works like grease and all the
ands become soft. When they are greased, then again the excretory matter does not
ck to them. After eating kichdi if possible do yoga nidra. Yoga nidra is like Shavasan.
this there is special importance of meditation. now the five asanas necessary for
urification of intestine are being given.

1. Urdhawatadasan

Urdhawatadasan

rocess :

Stand straight and interlock the fingers of both
the hands and keep them on the head. Keep the
legs close.

Inhale and stretch the hands in upward direction
and simultaneously lift the ankles. While exhaling
come down. Keep the hands on the head. Repeat
this 5 times.

Tiryak Tadasan

rocess :

Stand in the above mentioned position, take the
hands up, interlock the fingers and stretch them
straight upwards. The palms will be open towards
the sky, there will be a distance of one foot
between the legs.

2. While inhaling bend to the right, without bending backwards or forwards, bend as much as possible and bend the hands. The hands should not fold at the elbows. While exhaling take the hands above the head. In the same way do it on the left side. In this way do repetitions on each side.

3. Katichakrasan

Process :

Tiryak Tadasan

1. Keep a distance of one foot between the legs and stand straight. Spread both the hands along the shoulders, the palms should be straight facing the ground.

2. Turn the right hand from the front and keep it on the left shoulder. Fold the l(e) hand from the backside and keep it on the waist. The palm of the hand which on the waist will be towards upside.

3. Now turn the neck left and from the backside look at the right ankle. If you cannot see then just pretend seeing. After doing from one side repeat on the other side. In this way do 5 repetitions on each side.

Katichakrasan

Katichakrasan

Second process :

Stand up and bring both the hands in front of the chest. While inhaling turn the hands towards right side as much as possible. The distance between the hands should be equal to the chest and then look in between the hands. While exhaling come back to the middle position. In the same way do it form the other side.

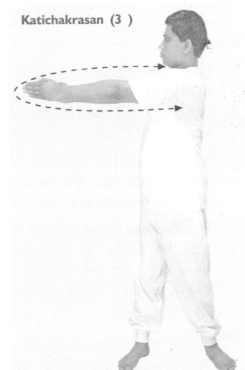
Katichakrasan (3)

4. Tiryak Bhujangasan

Process :

1. Lie down on your stomach and keep both the hands near the chest and shoulders, the elbows should be touching the sides and raised up.

2. There should be a distance of one foot between the legs. Stretch the paws towards back. While inhaling lift the chest. When the portion till below the navel area is raised, look at the left ankle from above the right shoulder. While exhaling come down. Repeat this from left side.

3. When the portion till below the navel area is raised, look at the left ankle from above the right shoulder. While exhaling come down. Repeat thes form left side.

Tiryak Bhujangasan

5. Udarakarshan or Shankhasan

Process:

1. Sit on your feet and keep both the hands on the knees. keep a distance of one foot between the legs.

2. While inhaling rest the right knee near the left paw and bend the left knee towards the right side.

3. Turn the neck to the left side from back. Remain in this position for some time and get back to the middle position. Repeat this from the other side.

Benefits:

1. This action as mentioned before cures all types of diseases.

2. The body becomes clean and pure and light like a flower and shines.

3. All types of stomach problems like stomach diseases, constipation, dysentery, gas, acidity, sour belches, piles etc. are definitely cured.

Shankhasan

4. It is extremely beneficial for obesity, diabetes, heart problem, appendicitis, headache, problems of mouth, throat, tongue and eyes.

5. It cures the menstrual disorders in females. Joint pain, arthritis, and other wind related problems, premature graying of the hair, wrinkles, pigmentation marks and other disorders.

6. It is beneficial in the disease of intestines, kidney, pancreas, and spleen. Whatever merits are told they are less.

Cautions :

1. In the beginning this should be practiced under the guidance of a master. While doing asana it will be tiring which can be painful.

2. In this purification process lukewarm water and salt is used. Asana practice increases thirst and heat. In such case if cold water is consumed it can be harmful and the body feels tired and weak. The person will feel unhealthy, for this it is necessary that in the beginning the temperature of the water should be normal and the quantity of salt should not be more. Next time the salt quantity can be increased and slowly practicing the exercise will solve the problems. If vomiting occurs on drinking water, drink less water and do not do Tiryak Bhujangasan.

3. At the first instance bowels will be passed. After that yellow water, after yellow water, water like bowel will be passed. After that again yellowish water will come out. Till then this process should be stopped.

4. After eating kichdi, water should not be taken till 3 hours. Even after three hours if you want to drink water, take hot water. Cold water should not be taken on that day. Because cold water can cause problems in the throat, and cause cold etc.

5. Rest for the whole day, do not get exposed to the wind, after the process, rest should be taken but do not sleep.

6. Do not take bath after the process. If it is summer season then hot water bath can be taken in the evening.

7. After the process, do not sit under the fan in summer season and under the Sun in winter season.

8. Do not wash the hands and legs with cold water for the whole day, this can cause swelling. On cloudy and rainy day this process should not be done.

9. Children, mother of a new born baby, and extremely weak persons should not do this.

10. After three days of action, milk and milk products like sweets, buttermilk, curd, etc, should not be taken.(except ghee)

11. The kichdi should be made by adding rice and dal in equal quantities. At the time of cooking only rock salt and turmeric powder is to be added. Do not use any other thing. The day this process is to be done only kichdi and ghee is to be taken. Do not eat any other thing. After this also, those who are obese, have indigestion problem, diabetes should have only kichdi till three

days. Ghee should not be added in the same quantity as in the previous time. Normally on the second day gourd, and other light vegetables can be taken. It implies that only easily digestible food items should be take and that too in less quantity. Slowly after three days take normal meals.

Time of practice :

Diabetics should do this activity once in 40 days. Patients of piles, chronic constipation and scorasis should do this once in 40 days. A healthy person should do this once in six months or once a year, so that no disease will affect.

Mild purification of the intestine (Laghu shankh prakshalan)

This is beneficial for patients of constipation due to indigestion, obesity and diabetes. In this case also hot water is taken and asanas are practiced. In this case only 7 to 8 glasses of water should be taken not more. This will pass the bowels three to four times and the stomach will be cleaned. After this if desired vaman dhouti can be done.

Note: The benefits are as mentioned before. In this case there is no need follow strict diet plan, after the activity take kichdi with ghee. In the evening chapati and vegetable can be taken. On the day this action is done it is better not to consume milk and buttermilk.

Ganesh Kriya(Basic purification)

Dip the index finger of the left hand in castor oil. Immerse it one inch deep in the rectum and turn it on all sides and remove the faecal matter. Wash the hand and repeat it again. In this way remove the other dirt matter present in the rectum. This process is done after passing the bowel. The fingers should not have nails. Cut the nails with the nail cutter and rub it nicely.

Benefits : This action strengthens the internal and external muscles of the rectum, which prevents constipation and other diseases. The remaining faces present in the rectum after passing the bowels comes out easily with this action, so that one does not have to suffer with diseases like piles etc. It is extremely beneficial for piles patients. They should do this exercise everyday.

3. Basti

Sucking the water or air through the rectum opening and purifying the large intestine is called basti. It is of two types- Jal basti and pavan basti. To expertise in this process it is necessary to practice *uddiyanbandh, vam dakhshin nouli* and *nouli madhyama.*

1. Jal basti

Process:

1. Stand in clean water up to the navel level and perform the process. This action can be done by filling a big tub and sitting in Utkatasan.

2. Sit in Utkatasan and take six to seven inches long wooden stick with a hole, both the edges of the stick should be smoothened and rounded off with some liquid and pierce it in the rectum opening. The other end of the stick should be in the water.

3. Exhale and perform *uddiyanbandh, moolbandh* and *nouli madhyama*. With this the water will be sucked till such time that you do not take breath.

4. Before inhaling close the other end of the stick with the finger. Again exhale and suck the water like before. Repeating this for 5 to 6 times will fill the large intestine with enough water.

5. Now remove the stick and stand up and do *nouli* action. With this the water will spread in the intestine and clean it.

6. When *nouli* is turned from the right side there will be a desire to pass the bowels, pass it.

7. This process can be done without the wooden pipe by standing in the water as mentioned before and doing *uddiyan bandh* and *moolbandh* and suck the water upwards. When *moolbandh* etc. are performed properly the rectum opening becomes wide and the water passes through it automatically. Add little lime juice in the water. This process should be done in the morning after getting free from bowels etc.

Benefits :

Basti purifies the large intestines, which cures constipation and other diseases, the heat of the stomach reduces, which cures dream problems and other humor related problems. This action is more beneficial than anima. In anima water is passed with pressure, in this case the large intestine is inactive. In this the large intestine expands and its natural strength is lost. Whereas in basti the intestine attracts water, which increases its strength rather than decreasing.

2) Pavanbasti

Sit in Utkatasan as mentioned before, exhale and perform *moolbandh, uddiyan bandh* and *nouli madhyama*. Fill the air inside. In this way filling the air inside and taking it outside is called pavan basti.

Benefits : Same as above. But in the previous case i.e., jal basti process faces comes out, and in this only polluted air comes out. Therefore this process is beneficial for wind related problems and piles. It also increases the fire of the stomach.

4. Tratak

Process:

1. Sit in any one of the meditative posture namely Padmasan, Sidhasan etc.

2. Burn a *diya* of ghee and keep it at a distance of 3 to 4 feet in front of the eyes. If ghee is not available mustard oil can be used.

3. Now without blinking your eyes glaze at the flame. *Diya* should be kept at a place where is no wind.

4. When tears start pouring or eyes start burning stop glazing. If tears starts rolling, then after some time dip your head and eyes in a vessel containing cold water and open your eyes. Bring the vessel near your face and open and close your eyes in the vessel. This will reduce the burning sensation of the eyes. The duration of practice should be increased gradually. If the practice lasts for three hours then the results are miraculous. This also creates different types of yogic accomplishments. The time which we spend for glazing the flame outside (known as external tratak), the same time should be spent for remembering the enlightened Supreme Soul, God by concentrating between the eyebrows. This accomplishes concentration and it is easy to enter the field of meditation. Glazing can be also be done by putting a black mark on a white paper. Tratak is also done by glazing at the Moon and the rising Sun. The guidance of an expert should be taken in order to accomplish the act of glazing completely.

Benefits:

1. This completely eliminates the inattentiveness of the mind, which gives easy entry into tithe fields of Yoga.

2. It increase the eyesight.

3. You don't see dreams when Tratak is performed in the evening and even if the dreams come they are very few. Tratak gives sound sleep and protects from bad dreams.

5. Nouli

Nouli Madhyama:

Process :

1. Keeping a distance of one to one and half foot distance between the legs, keep the hands on the knees and stand up. Press the knees with the hands. Look at the ground.

2. In the beginning some difficulty will be faced while performing nouli, therefore first Agnisar must be done in order to expertise in Nouli. Exhale fully and contract the stomach to an extent that the stomach attaches with the back, then expand the stomach. Repeat this according to capacity. This will soften the stomach and will be helpful in doing nouli process.

3. Now for doing nouli stand in the previous position. Pressing the knees, contract the stomach from the side and expand the center portion and try to expand both the muscles in the front.

4. When you feel like inhaling, inhale and repeat the exercise.

Vam nouli: (left side)

Process : Stand in the previous position and perform nouli madhyama. When nouli comes in center bend forward and put pressure on the left hand, this will bring forward the left muscle out of the big muscles of the stomach. the right side should be left loose in this case.

Vam Nouli

Dakshin nouli:(right nouli)

Process: Dakshin (right) nouli is same like vam (left) nouli, the procedure is same as right nouli.

Nouli circulation:

Process: When the nouli performs in both the directions, then extend the stomach outside and massage the thighs with the hands in other words rotate the palms up and down. When you do this you will see the stomach starts rotating from right to left. Practice may take some time. After doing from the right side do it from the left side.

Benefits:

1. *Hathyoga Pradipika* describes stomach action to be the top most among all the actions." 'हठ क्रिया मौलिरियं च नौलिं।'

2. It definitely cures dysentery, constipation, gas, chronic disorder of the bowels, obesity of the stomach and other stomach problems.

3. It is also beneficial in gynecological problems, painful menstruation etc.

4. This is the important action for kundilini yoga, where in the outgoing air and incoming air are controlled.

Caution: Those who have slipdisc, heart problem and ulcer should not attempt this.

6. Kapalbhati

Process : Sit in Padmasan or Sidhasan and keep both the hands on the knees. Inhale and push the lower portion of the navel area towards the backside and divide the air in various parts and take it out. At the end take out all the air and do *mahabandh*. Repeat the exercise again. In one minute 60 pushes should be given. After that it can be increased up to 120 times. A beginner should do it 25 to 30 times in a minute.

Benefits : This exercise is the purifier of the brain hence known as kapal bhati. 'Bha dipto" means one which enlightens the brain. It is beneficial for the lungs and heart. Liver, intestines and pancreas and complete digestive system benefits from this and it increases blood circulation.

Subject of Mudra

Yoga devotion gives special importance to mudras other than eight yogic practices. Mudras are the developed forms of asanas. In asanas senses are primary and prana is secondary, whereas in mudras senses are secondary and pranas is primary. The classics describe the importance of mudra and say: नास्ति मुद्रासमं किंचित् सिद्धिदं क्षितिमंडले, this means there is no other action on this earth which gives the same results as of mudras. For convenience the various mudras are being described under two topics.

1. Hand mudraa controlling the elements.
2. Mudras helpful in awakening the kundilini and soul.

Hand mudra controlling the elements.

The whole universe is created with five elements. Our body is also made of five elements. The five fingers of our body denote the five elements. The thumb fire, index finger represents air, middle finger represents space / sky, ring finger represents earth and little finger represents water. The body remains healthy with the balance between the five elements and in adverse conditions diseases are caused. According to the science of bodily actions(mudra) the balanced action of these five elements controls the internal glands, body parts, and their functions and the dormant powers of the body are awakened.

The actions of the hand start functioning instantly. The hand in which the mudras are made, they start affecting in the opposite part at the same instance. These mudras can be done either while standing, sitting or walking. It is more beneficial to sit in Vajrasan, Padmasan or Sukhasan and do the hand actions. In the beginning they can be practiced for 10 minutes and later on practiced up to 30 to 45 minutes to get complete benefit. If you cannot do all at once then do it in three or four times. While doing any action the finger that is not being used should be kept straight.

I. Gyan or Dhyan Mudra : Touch the thumb and index finger with each other and keep the remaining three fingers straight.

Benefits :

1. It develops concentration and meditation stage. It increases attentiveness and removes negative thinking.

2. It increases the memory power, therefore the children become intelligent and sharp minded with the regular practice of this mudra.

3. The brain nerves become strong. It cures insomnia, headache and stress. It destroys anger and for better results perform prana mudra after this mudra.

Vayu Mudra   Gyan Mudra

II. Vayu mudra : Join the index finger to the tip of the thumb and put slight pressure with the thumb, then it becomes vayu mudra. the remaining three fingers should be kept straight.

Benefits : Regular practice of this mudra eliminates all wind related problems like - arthritis, joint pain, gout, paralysis, vertigo, sciatica, knee pain and gas formation stops. It also benefits in the pain of the neck and spine. It cures the impurities in blood circulation.

III. Shunya mudra: the middle finger represents space/sky, joint this finger to the tip of the thumb and put slight pressure with the thumb. The remaining fingers should be kept straight.

Benefits : This mudra cures secretion from the ears, ear pain, deafness or hearing problem if practiced for long time or at least one hour daily. It cures heart problem and weakness in the bones. The gums become strong and it also benefits in throat and thyroid problems.

Caution : Do not do this mudra while eating & waking.

Shunya Mudra

Prithivi Mudra

IV. Prithvi mudra: Join the tips of ring finger and thumb and keep the remaining three fingers straight, this makes prithvi mudra.

Benefits: Regular practice cures weakness of the body, leanness, obesity and other diseases. This mudra improves digestion power, develops the life power and pious qualities. and cures the deficiency of the vitamins. It makes the body active, fit and vigour.

V. Prana Mudra: This mudra is formed by joining the tips of little finger, ring finger and thumb. The remaining two fingers should be kept straight.

Benefits: The dormant power of life is awakened, develops health, activity and energy in the body. It cures the eye problems and increases the eye sight. It increases the immunity system of the body, cures the deficiency of vitamins and removes weakness and circulates new energy, rejuvenates the body. During long hours of fasting, one does not feel hungry and thirsty. During insomnia it should be done along with gyan mudra.

VI. Apan mudra: This mudra is made by joining the tips of thumb, ring finger and middle finger and keeping the remaining two fingers straight.

Benefits : It removes the foreign particles from the body, and the body becomes pure. Practicing this mudra cures constipation, Wind related problems, diabetes, urination problem, kidney problem, tooth problems and other diseases. It is beneficial for the stomach. It helps in heart problem and brings perspiration.

Caution: This mudra will cause excess urination.

Pran Mudra   Apan Mudra   Apan Vayu Mudra

VII. Apan vayu mudra : Performing apan mudra and vayu mudra together creates apan vayu mudra. The little finger remains straight.

Benefits : It cures heart and wind related problems and makes the body healthy. Those who have weak heart should practice this regularly. In case of heart attack, performing this mudra gives immediate relief. It releases gas accumulated in the stomach. It is beneficial in headache, asthma and high blood pressure. Performing this mudra 5 to 7 minutes before climbing up the stairs is beneficial.

VIII. Surya Mudra : Keep the ring finger on the lower portion of the thumb and press it gently with the thumb.

Benefits : This balances the body, reduces weight, reduces obesity and increases heat in the body which helps in proper digestion. It reduces stress, develops strength and reduces cholesterol content in the blood. Practicing this mudra cures diabetes and liver problems.

Caution : This should not be performed by a weak person. Do not stay in heat for a long time.

Varun Mudra   Surya Mudra

Yog Sadhna
&
Yoga Healing Secrets

IX. Varun mudra: Join the little finger with the thumb.

Benefits: This mudra removes dryness of the body, makes the skin soft, smooth and gives shine. It cures skin disorders, pimples, acne, and diseases which are caused due to deficiency of water element. It makes the face beautiful.

Caution : People with phlegm constitution should not practice this.

Ling Mudra

X. Ling mudra : Interlock the fingers as shown in the picture and keep the thumb of the left hand straight, the other fingers should be interlocked tightly.

Benefits : This mudra increases heat. It is beneficial in cold-, asthma, cough, sinuses, paralysis, and low blood pressure. This dries the phlegm.

Caution: Do not consume water, fruits, fruit juices, ghee, milk in excess quantity. Do not practice this for long time.

XI. Dharna shakti mudra: This mudra stops the breath in the lungs for longer time. When you do purak (inhaling), then press the first part (lower portion) of the thumb with the index finger, this helps in performing kumbhak for a longer time. If you press the middle portion of the thumb then kumbhak can be done for still longer time, In case the first part (upper portion) of the thumb is pressed then kumbhak can be done very long time easily.

Dharna Shakti Mudra

Benefits: The prana air remains in the lungs for a longer time, they get more of that air and the body and the blood get more strength and the breath taken in the whole day can be reduced, which increases the longevity.

Mudras beneficial in awakening of kundilini and prana

I. Bhachuri mudra : Sitting in Padmasan or Sidhasan or in any other meditative pose and looking at the open sky from a distance of roughly two inches and stabilising the mind is Bhachuri Mudra.

Benefits : It increases attentiveness and makes the mind suitable of meditation.

2. Khechari mudra : Folding the tongue in the reverse side and touching the palate is called Khechari Mudra. This mudra should be practiced under the guidance of a master.

Benefits : In yoga classics the benefits of this mudra have been described excessively. In the yoga tradition it is considered that regular practice of this mudra, the yogi starts getting the flavor of nectar. With the practice of Khechari Mudra, the nectar juice(sweet juice) secrets from the nectar glands. The devotee does not feel hungry, thirsty and sleepy.

3. Ashwini mudra : Sit in padmasan or Vajrasan or any other meditative pose and contracting and expanding the rectum opening is called Ashwini Mudra. This can be practiced while sleeping, sitting, or in any other position at any time, anywhere. Performing this mudra after doing bahya kumbhak is more beneficial. Begin with 20 to 25 times and extend it till 50 to 100 times.

Benefits :

1. It is beneficial in celibacy and awakening of the prana.

2. It cures the gas, constipation, piles and urinary problems and makes the rectum area healthy.

3. Practicing this mudra keeps the genitals of both male and female healthy and free of problems. The female uterus remains healthy and strong. If the pregnant lady practices this the delivery is performed easily.

4. Yoni mudra : Sit in Sidhasan and first inhale and then press the both the ears with the thumb of both the hands, both the eyes with the index fingers, both the nostrils with middle fingers, both the holes of the nose with the ring fingers and lips with the little fingers. In this way close all the openings and chant Omkar mantra in the mind and concentrate the mind and determine that the energy is producing from below and reaching the lotus shaped heart. This is also called Parangmuhi mudra.

Benefits : The prana and apana air join together and help in awakening the kundilini. The condition of appearance of the chakras take place and a divine light is formed.

5. Unmani Mudra : Sit in Padmasan and look in between the eyebrows and concentrate in the agya chakra. Do not allow any thoughts to come into your mind and concentrate only on the agya chakra.

Benefits : This mudra is beneficial in concentration and meditation, the mind and all the senses become insensitive, which cause the condition of resistance of senses and mind becomes stable and the condition of deep meditation takes place. The light of knowledge originates and the person experiences the truth.

Shakti chalini mudra : As the urine bladder is pulled inside to stop the urge of urination, in the same way sitting in vajrasan and pulling the urinary bladder inside is called shakti chalini mudra. In the beginning it should be done for 20 to 25 times and slowly increased to 50 to 100 times.

benefits: the problems, of laziness, carelessness and stupidity are cured. It awakens the prana very soon and the kundilini rises, as a result the path of science o chakra opens. practice of this mudra by females keeps their uterus and reproductive organs healthy.

7. Vipreet Karani Mudra:

Lie down straight on your back. Then join both the legs and keep them straight and raise them and support the waist with the hands. Raise the legs straight not towards the roof but slightly downwards, In Sarvangasan the legs are raised up to 90 degrees straight. Whereas in this mudra the legs are at an angle of 45 degrees, in the position of Ardhasarvangasan. Then perform *jalandhar bandh* and look at the big toes. Breathe normally. Begin with 10 minutes and then slowly increase the duration.

Vipreet Karni Mudra

Benefits: Regular practice of this exercise gives all the benefits of Sarvangasan, increases the fire of the stomach. It increases the appetite, make s the body healthy, brings shine on the face and the premature graying of hair does not take place. Mental strength increases. Swelling of the legs, the beginning stage of elephantiasis, goiter, boils, pimples, eczema and blood impurities generated diseases are cured. This is especially beneficial in purification of the intestine and while doing purification process, if the water does not come out of the rectum opening then with this mudra water from small intestine to the large intestine flows easily and slowly starts coming out, which cleans the stomach.

8. Yoga mudra : With this practice the body remains healthy, fit, flexible and the nerves are purified and the pranas get strength. The internal soul becomes pure. It helps in the stages of concentration, meditation and deep meditation. For the procedure and picture refer yoga mudrasan 1 and 2 given on pg 52.

9. Mudrasan : Keep the left ankle in between the rectum and the genital firmly and stretch the right leg. Then gradually along with purak perform *jalandhar bandh* and *mool bandh* and place the left leg toe on the right knee and perform kumbhak as per capacity. (While doing kumbhak blow the air in the stomach after purak imagine that the prana kunidlini is awakening and entering the ray of the Sun). After that lift the forehead slowly from the knee while doing rechak and sit in the original position. In the same way repeat it with the other leg. Increase the time of pranayam and repetitions.

Benefits : According to Goraksha system the diseases like tuberculosis, leprosy, boils near the kidney, indigestion, stomach problems, disease in which the vital humors of the body are secreted through urine are cured with this mudra. Practicing this for a longer time helps the pranas to enter the ray of Sun, and the pranas travel upward and kundilini rises.

10. Tribandh mudra : Sit in padmasan and do purak and mix the outgoing breath and lift the outgoing breath from the lower portion of the navel and perform *jalandhar bandh, uddiyan bandh, moolbandh* and try the internal air to enter the ray of Sun. Remain in this position and keep the palms on both the sides and keep on lifting the hips and slowly rest them on the ground, do this several times.

Benefits : The prana starts entering the ray of Sun very soon. The kundilini awakens very soon and starts moving upward, the chakara also start enlightening slowly.

11. Brahma mudra: Sit in Vajrasan, rotate the head and shoulders upwards-downwards, right-left, and in circular motion, and then on all the four sides. Repeat each exercise 5 to 10 times.

Benefits: Vertigo, cervical spondalitis, stiffness of the neck are cured. With his practice throat problems do not occur, headache stops and the brain nerves become strong.

12. Agnisar Kriya: Sit in Vajrasan or stand up and exhale and move the stomach forwards and backwards. Till such time that you can do bahya kumbhak, contract and expand the stomach area till the navel area and repeat this at least 20 to 40 times. Do not move the shoulders. Then take deep breath 4 to 5 times and again repeat this exercise. In this way do this 4 to 5 times as per capacity.

Benefits:

1. Indigestion does not take place even after sitting in deep meditation for a long time. The digestion takes place smoothly, it cures constipation, gas, belch and other stomach related problems. It increases the appetite.

2. Obesity, diabetes and urine problem are improved. The burning sensation in the urine reduces. This action stops diabetes.

Acupressure treatment

Putting pressure on the special points situated in the human body and curing the disease is called acupressure. The word Acupressure means pressure. Putting pressure on the special fixed points in the body and different diseases are cured in a miraculous manner with this medication

Principle of Acupressure.

According to this system each disease is cured by treating the physical and psychological forms as one combined unit. In acupressure system the human body is considered to be an integral unit of the psychological body.

The second most important principle is that main points of all the blood circulating nerves, nervous system, glands are situated in the center part of the palms, and feet. In this system, the pressure points located in different parts are put pressure and from there the energy is circulated to the all the nerves, nervous system and glands and made healthy. Uncontrolled and imbalanced food, laziness-carelessness and sleepiness and rules related to celibacy when violated, foreign particles get accumulated in the body and lack of asana and pranayam etc the body organs start becoming inactive. The muscles become weak, the bones of the spine and hands and legs start shifting from their position. The functioning of the entire nervous system starts reducing. The blood circulation in the physical organs starts decreasing. The chemical elements, toxic substances, foreign particles deposited in the blood start collecting near the joints. The more the number of such accumulation, the more the number of diseases. As the functioning of the body parts starts reducing the related pressure points situated on the palms and feet also start getting blocked and some kind of minute chemical item collects on the points, due to which the blood circulation in the related parts does not take place properly. With Acupressure system, the pressure is given on those points and the crystal deposits are destroyed., due to which the blood circulation is regulated and the afflicted organs become healthy. According to another principle, our body is made out of five elements. the five elements - earth, fire, wind, water and space/sky are regulated with an electric power which is called bio-electricity or bio-energy. According to the famous acupressure practitioner F.M.Thestan (The healing benefits of Acupressure) when the pressure is put on the different pressure points situated in the body, hands and legs, pain is experienced, from there the related organs are leaking and in other words going out of the body. As a result the related body organs have some problem or the other. When we put pressure on these points, the electricity does not go out. With the stoppage of leakage, the electric power supply to the related body organs becomes normal and the diseases are cured.

Main effects of Acupressure on the human body

1. With the acupressure system the foreign particles are removed out of the body and the important elements are produced with the internal immunity system.

2. This method raises the electric powers of the body and creates energy and activity.

3. It creates flexibility in all the muscular tissues of the body.

4. It cures the deformities in the bones and spine.

5. Acupressure is fully helpful in curing the nervous system problems.

6. With this system the thyroid, pituitary, pineal, pancreas and other glands are controlled.

7. With acupressure the normal functioning of the internal organs can be improved to a considerable extent.

Acupressure - Indian Knowledge

Acupressure is the improved version of Indian deep massage system, which means curing the diseases by putting pressure on some important points of hand, legs, face and body. Acupressure has not been imported from China and other countries. In fact, the Chinese invaders who came to visit India, took the ancient Indian Ayurvedic texts and propagated that acupressure is their science and spread it in the entire world.

Treating this as a foreign science is extremely unlucky. Acupressure has extensive description in the Indian classics. Why do the Indian women used to wearing anklets, toe rings, bangles, pendants, tika(ornament put on the forehead), earrings, pierce their nose and wear small studs and waist chain, this needs to be analyzed. Men and women are wearing rings for a long time. This is all because of acupressure.

Treatment of main diseases with acupressure

Though acupressure has a special utility in all the disease, this a harmless system and this can be adopted along with other medication systems. But there are few diseases, which can be successfully treated with acupressure, which have been described below:

1. World Health Organization(WHO) has accepted the utility of acupressure and acupuncture medication system and has accepted that this treatment is more beneficial for sciatica, cervical, spondalitis, spinal problems, frozen shoulders, knee pain, bed wetting, ulcer, piles, constipation, headache, migraine, deformity of nerves-veins, gas formation, acidity, swelling of the throat, tonsils, sinusitis, bronchitis,

asthma, ear, nose, throat problems, teeth pain, paralysis, minors disease and other diseases.

2. We have applied the acupressure treatment system on thousands of patients in the Brahmakalp hospital managed by the ashram to cure the above mentioned diseases. Several times the patients have obtained miraculous benefits. When the patients were unable to turn their necks due to severe cervical spondalitis pain, we treated them within 5 to 10 minutes. Chronic shoulder pain, in which the it was not possible to move and rotate the neck, in that situation we have completely cured the problem within 5 to 10 minutes. In our opinion in all types of physical pains, joint pains and backache and deformities of the nerves and veins, the instant relief which acupressure gives, no other system gives that instant relief.

3. In case of heart pain also acupressure gives quick relief and the blockage in the arteries is cured.

4. This is also useful in stomach problems, diabetes and brain related problems.

5. Along with curing the disease, we consider acupressure to be an important system of diagnosis of the disease. With this system pressure is laid on different pressure points and it can be easily found out that which parts of the body or organs and glands are unable to function properly. Many a times the diagnostic centers are unable to detect the exact cause of the diseases. In this situation by testing the pressure points within seconds it can be found out which organ has the disease, in this situation the pressure points are known as the mirror the diseases.

Testing of the pressure points and method of giving pressure:

1. Acupressure can be done with thumb, stick, plastic equipment and any other suitable thing according to convenience.

2. Neither put excess pressure nor too less pressure on the points. In fact medium pressure should be given. While doing this if anybody has unbearable pain in the pressure points that means the organ related to the point is diseased. The points which do not experience pain they should be considered to be healthy.

3. when pressure is laid on the points the foreign particles and crystals deposited in the blood flowing veins and nerves leave their position and start flowing and then excreted through urine with the functioning of the kidneys. For this reason while doing acupressure after pressing the desired points, the points of kidney should be pressed for one or two minutes. As the crystals leave their place with pressure, the speed of the disease also reduces and the patient experiences

benefit in the diseases. Applying this for some time regularly cures the diseases and the pain due to pressure either reduces or stops totally.

4. In the beginning when the pressure is laid on the points, most of the patients experience severe pain or swelling in the areas because the crystals start moving from their place . In this situation one should not feel afraid, this a natural action. If this happens, fomentation with lukewarm water added with salt should be done, which relieves pain and swelling.

Time of Acupressure

Normally acupressure can be done at anytime but incase of stomach, pancreas, bladder, liver etc. pressure should be given two three hours either before meals or after meals. Pressure should not be given immediately after taking meals because the body energy is consumed for digesting the food, therefore it is better to give acupressure before meals. Acupressure can be done after taking fruits or milk.

Duration of Pressure

According to the diseases, the pressure should be given on the related points for 30 seconds to 2 minutes. While putting pressure on any point the tolerance capacity of the patient should also be taken into account, other wise many times the patient faints. Same point should not be pressed again and again, in fact the pressure points should be changed and given on different points turn by turn. Normally pressure should be given twice a day, morning and evening. Incase of extreme pain acupressure can be done thrice a day.

Number of Pressure Points

Chenchuyu Su Eh (Ancient Chinese Acupressure) authored by Dr.Chu Li Yen is considered to be the authentic text possessed on this subject. This includes a list of 669 acupressure points. In other charts 1000 points have been shown. However in daily application around 100 points are only more useful.

The acupressure points situated in different parts of the body and which are useful for different diseases have been shown in the pictures in the next pages. These pictures have been compiled from a book called "Natural Acupressure Treatment" written by Dr. Uttar Singh.

Yog Sadhna
&
Yoga Healing Secrets

145

Width division of body in three parts

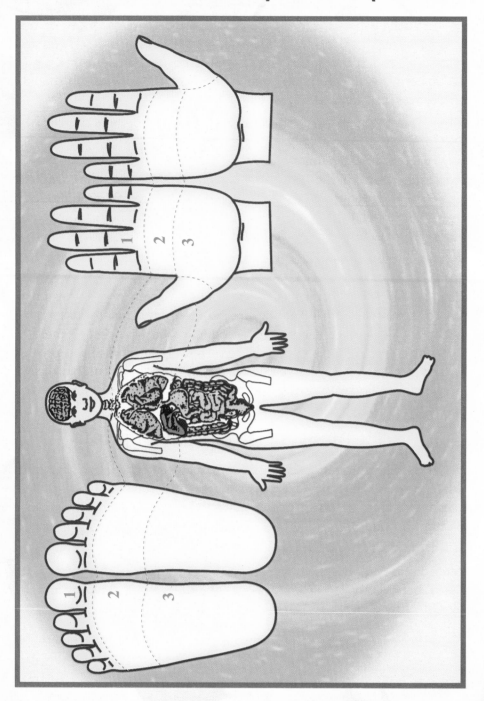

Main acupressure points situated in the hands

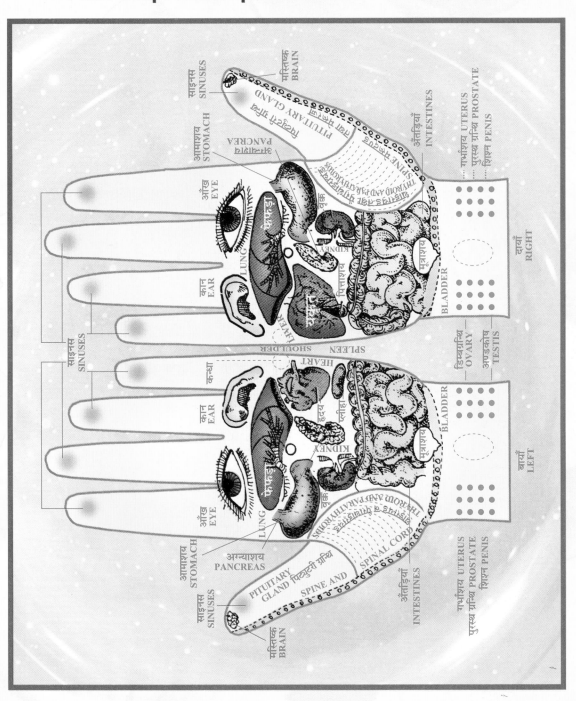

Main acupressure reflection point is feet.

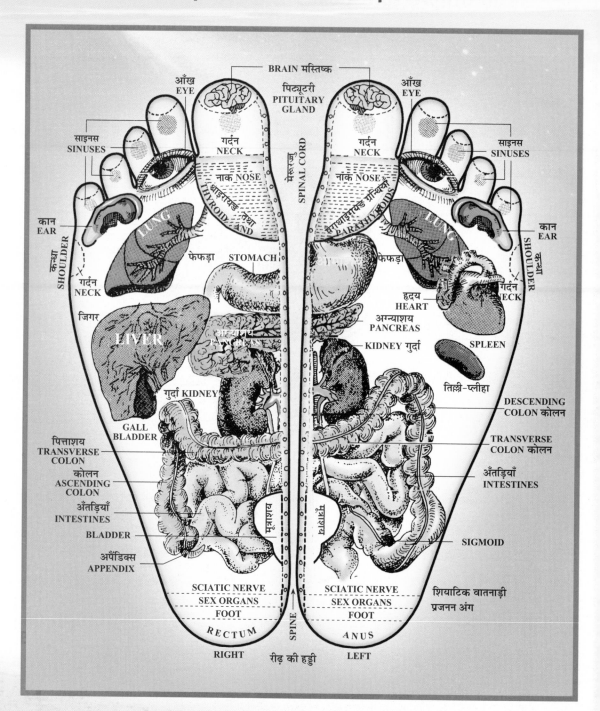

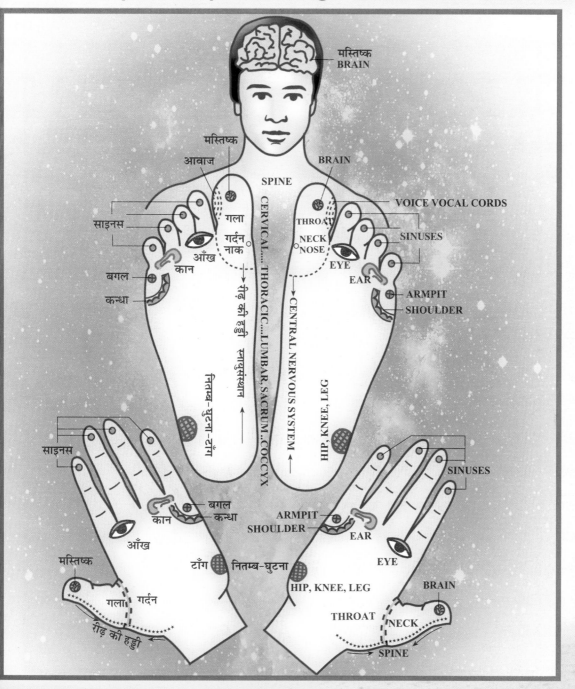

Position of Endocrine System in the body and its related pressure points situated in legs and hands

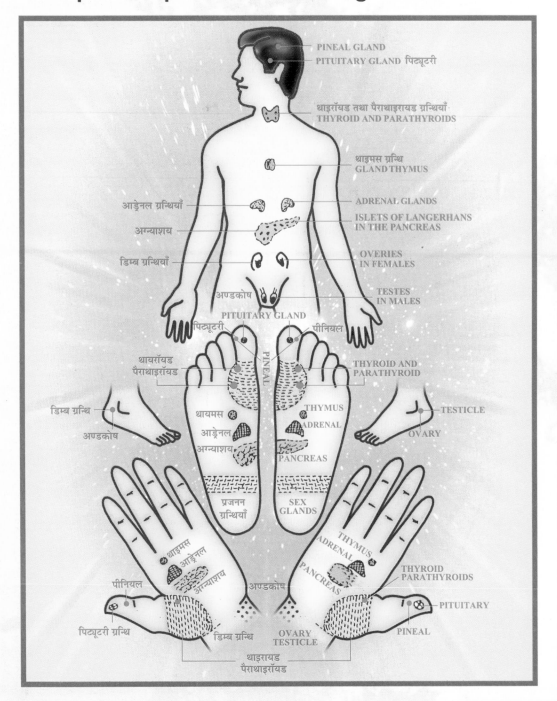

PINEAL GLAND
PITUITARY GLAND पिट्यूटरी

थाइरॉयड तथा पैराथाइरायड ग्रन्थियाँ
THYROID AND PARATHYROIDS

थाइमस ग्रन्थि
GLAND THYMUS

आड्रेनल ग्रन्थियाँ
ADRENAL GLANDS

अग्न्याशय
ISLETS OF LANGERHANS
IN THE PANCREAS

डिम्ब ग्रन्थियाँ
OVERIES
IN FEMALES

अण्डकोष
TESTES
IN MALES

PITUITARY GLAND
पिट्यूटरी
पीनियल

थायरॉयड
पैराथाइरॉयड
PINEAL
THYROID AND
PARATHYROID

डिम्ब ग्रन्थि
अण्डकोष

थायमस
आड्रेनल
अग्न्याशय
THYMUS
ADRENAL
PANCREAS

TESTICLE
OVARY

प्रजनन
ग्रन्थियाँ
SEX
GLANDS

थाइमस
आड्रेनल
अग्न्याशय
THYMUS
ADRENAL
PANCREAS

THYROID
PARATHYROIDS

पीनियल
अण्डकोष
PITUITARY

पिट्यूटरी ग्रन्थि
डिम्ब ग्रन्थि
OVARY
TESTICLE
PINEAL

थायरायड
पैराथाइरॉयड

Yog Sadhna
&
Yoga Healing Secrets

Position of heart and spleen in the body and its related pressure points situated in legs and hands

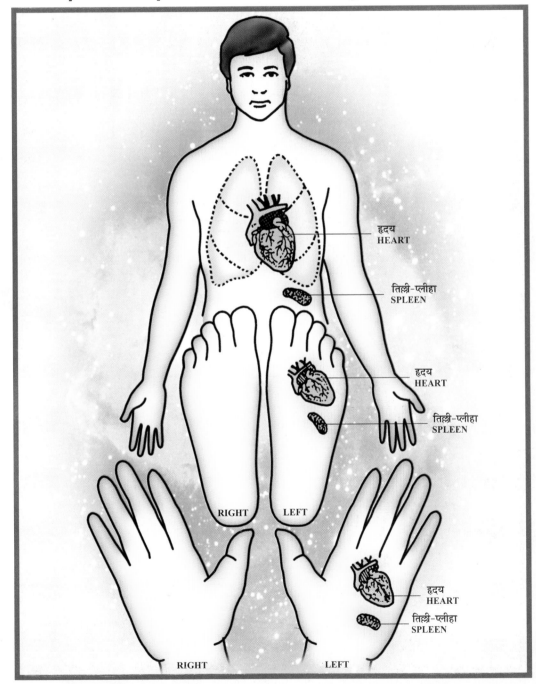

हृदय
HEART

तिल्ली-प्लीहा
SPLEEN

हृदय
HEART

तिल्ली-प्लीहा
SPLEEN

RIGHT   LEFT

हृदय
HEART

तिल्ली-प्लीहा
SPLEEN

RIGHT   LEFT

Position of different parts of respiratory system in the body and its related pressure points situated in legs and hands

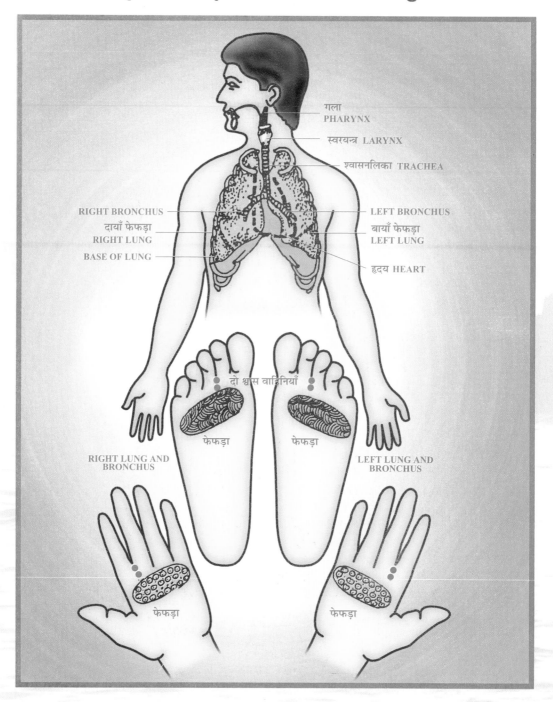

गला PHARYNX

स्वरयन्त्र LARYNX

श्वासनलिका TRACHEA

RIGHT BRONCHUS
दायाँ फेफड़ा
RIGHT LUNG

BASE OF LUNG

LEFT BRONCHUS
बायाँ फेफड़ा
LEFT LUNG

हृदय HEART

दो श्वास वाहिनियाँ

फेफड़ा   फेफड़ा

RIGHT LUNG AND
BRONCHUS

LEFT LUNG AND
BRONCHUS

फेफड़ा   फेफड़ा

Yog Sadhna
&
Yoga Healing Secrets

osition of different parts of digestive system in the body-liver,
ll bladder, stomach and intestine etc and the related pressure
points situated in the legs and hands

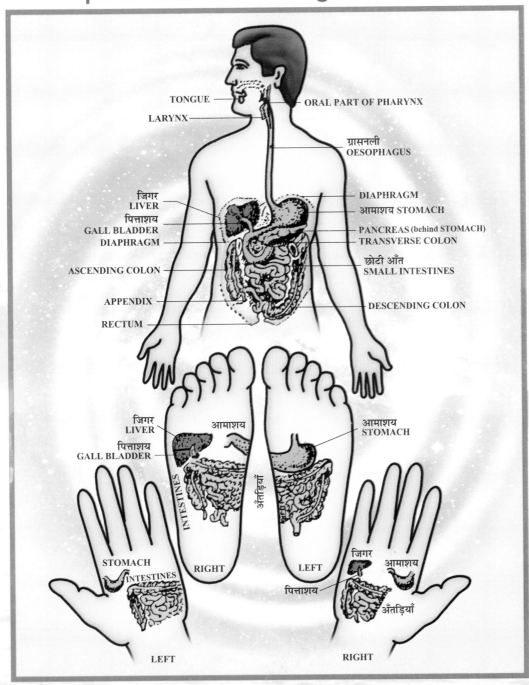

TONGUE — — ORAL PART OF PHARYNX
LARYNX —

ग्रासनली
OESOPHAGUS

जिगर
LIVER — — DIAPRAGM
पित्ताशय — — आमाशय STOMACH
GALL BLADDER
DIAPHRAGM — — PANCREAS (behind STOMACH)
— TRANSVERSE COLON
ASCENDING COLON — छोटी आँत
SMALL INTESTINES

APPENDIX — — DESCENDING COLON
RECTUM —

जिगर
LIVER — आमाशय — आमाशय
STOMACH
पित्ताशय
GALL BLADDER —

INTESTINES अँतड़ियाँ

STOMACH
INTESTINES
RIGHT LEFT जिगर आमाशय

पित्ताशय
अँतड़ियाँ

LEFT RIGHT

Position of different parts of urinary system in the body kidney ureters and bladder and the related pressure points situated the legs and hands

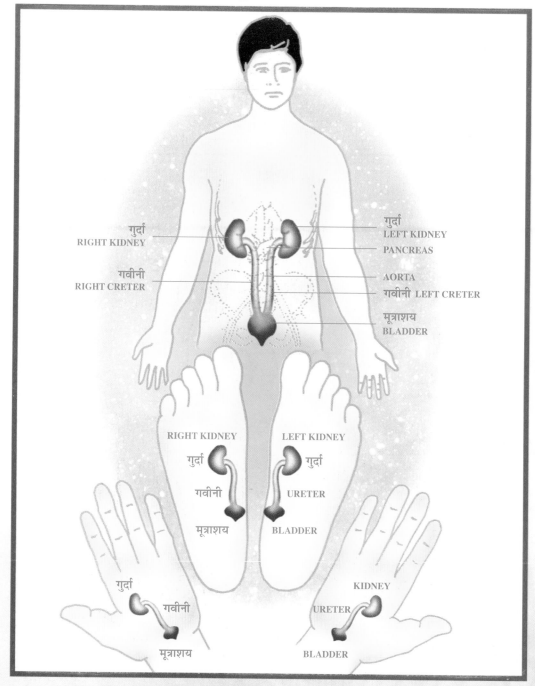

गुर्दा
RIGHT KIDNEY

गुर्दा
LEFT KIDNEY
PANCREAS

गवीनी
RIGHT CRETER

AORTA
गवीनी LEFT CRETER

मूत्राशय
BLADDER

RIGHT KIDNEY
गुर्दा

LEFT KIDNEY
गुर्दा

गवीनी

URETER

मूत्राशय

BLADDER

गुर्दा

गवीनी

KIDNEY

URETER

मूत्राशय

BLADDER

Yog Sadhna
&
Yoga Healing Secrets

Position of different parts of males and females reproductive system and the related pressure points situated in legs (Upper Side) feet, palms and wrist

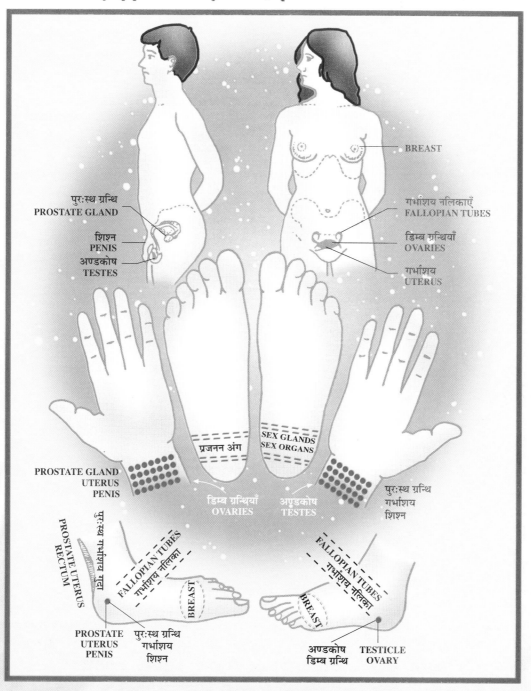

BREAST

पुर:स्थ ग्रन्थि
PROSTATE GLAND

शिश्न
PENIS

अण्डकोष
TESTES

गर्भाशय नलिकाएँ
FALLOPIAN TUBES

डिम्ब ग्रन्थियाँ
OVARIES

गर्भाशय
UTERUS

प्रजनन अंग

SEX GLANDS
SEX ORGANS

PROSTATE GLAND
UTERUS
PENIS

डिम्ब ग्रन्थियाँ
OVARIES

अण्डकोष
TESTES

पुर:स्थ ग्रन्थि
गर्भाशय
शिश्न

PROSTATE UTERUS RECTUM

पुर:स्थ गर्भाशय मलद्वार

FALLOPIAN TUBES
गर्भाशय नलिका

BREAST

FALLOPIAN TUBES
गर्भाशय नलिका

BREAST

PROSTATE
UTERUS
PENIS

पुर:स्थ ग्रन्थि
गर्भाशय
शिश्न

अण्डकोष
डिम्ब ग्रन्थि

TESTICLE
OVARY

Yog Sadhna
&
Yoga Healing Secrets

155

Various pressure points on the upper portion of the leg both the legs have equal points

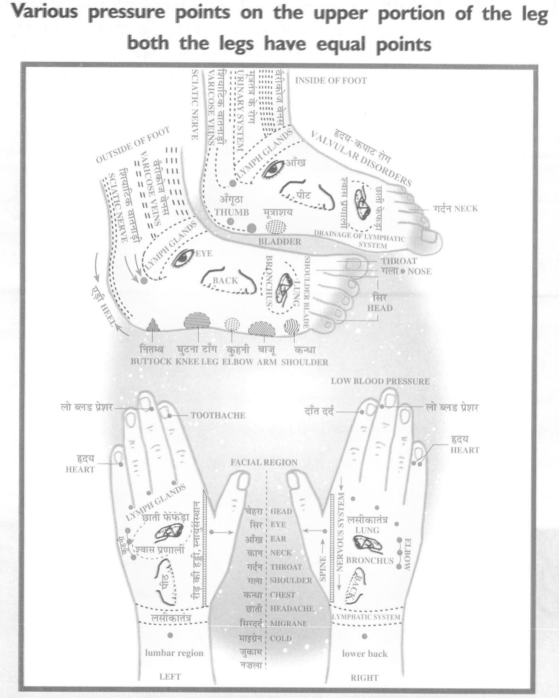

Various pressure points on the upper side of the hand both the hands have equal points

Inaddition to pressure points of liver, heart and spleen the acupressure treatment centers are some in both the legs

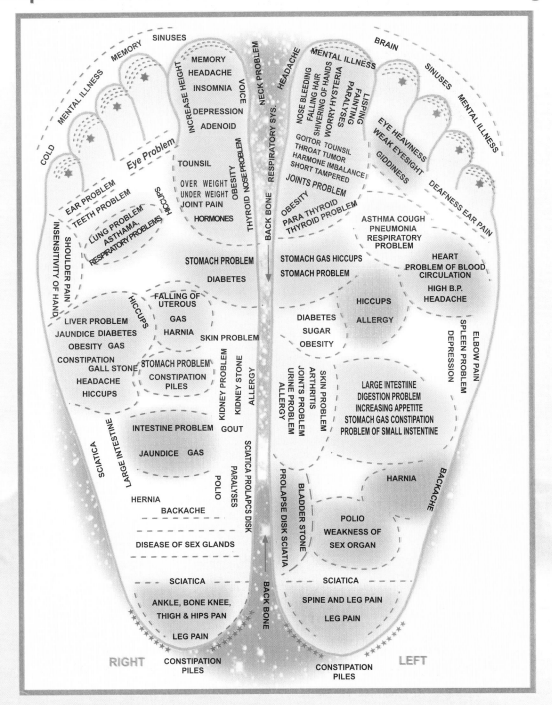

Different acupressure points situated on the face

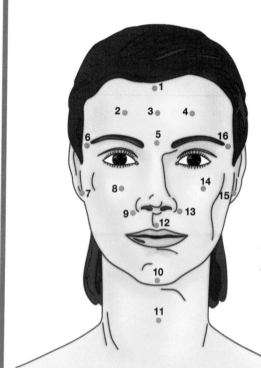

According to the diseases apply deep but light pressure on eash pressure point with the big finger or fingers up to 5-10 seconds.

1. (menstrual troubles)
2. 4, 8, 9, 13,14 (catarrh-headcold)
3. (pelvis troubles)
5. (headache, giddiness)
6. (severe headache)
7. (sleep disturbances) (paralysis)
10. (menopause complaints)
11. (throat, cough, dyspnea
    and asthma)
12. (tooth-ache)

Yog Sadhna
&
Yoga Healing Secrets

Different pressure points situated on the face

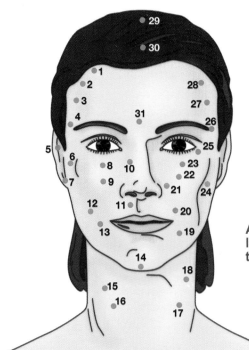

According to the diseases apply deep but light pressure on eash pressure point with the big finger or fingers up to 5-10 seconds.

● 1. Memory ● 2. Sciatica ● 3. and ● 25. Gas ● 4. Liver Problems ● 5. Blood Pressure ● 6. and ● 24. Tumour in the Throat ● 7. Paralysis ● 8. Kidney Problem ● 9, 14, 22. Constipation ● 10. Intestine Problem ● 11. Disease of Pancreas ● 12, 13. Disease related to the right Lung ● 15, 18. Erection ● 13, 17. Abdomen Problem ● 19, 20. Diseases related to the left Lung ● 23. Kidney Problems ● 26. Diseases of Spleen ● 27. Heart Problem ● 28. Sicatica ● 29. Severe Headache ● 30 Diseases related to the Sex Organs ● 31 Headache

Different acupressure points situated on the face

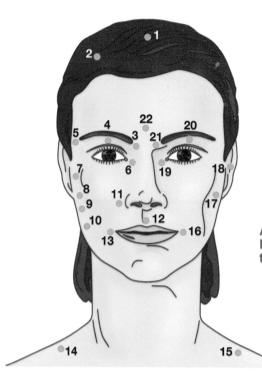

According to the diseases apply deep but light pressure on eash pressure point with the big finger or fingers up to 5-10 seconds.

● 1. Piles, Bladder Problems, Bed wettinig ● 2. Double vision diplipia ● 3. and ● 21. Brain problem, cold, insomnia ● 4, 20. Sciatica, Brain, Liver and Gall Bladder Diseases ● 5. Eye Problem ● 6, 14, 15, 19. Eye Problem ● 7. Hearing Problem ● 8, 10. Mental Stress & Paralysis ● 9, 17. Teeth's pain ● 11. Blockage in Nose, running Nose ● 12. Paralysis, Sneezing, fainting, Unconsciousness ● 13, 16. Toothache, Mental Stress ● 18. High Blood Pressue, Stiffness and pain in hands ● 22. Diseases of Eye's Legs and Stomach

Yog Sadhna
&
Yoga Healing Secrets

Different acupressure points situated on the ears

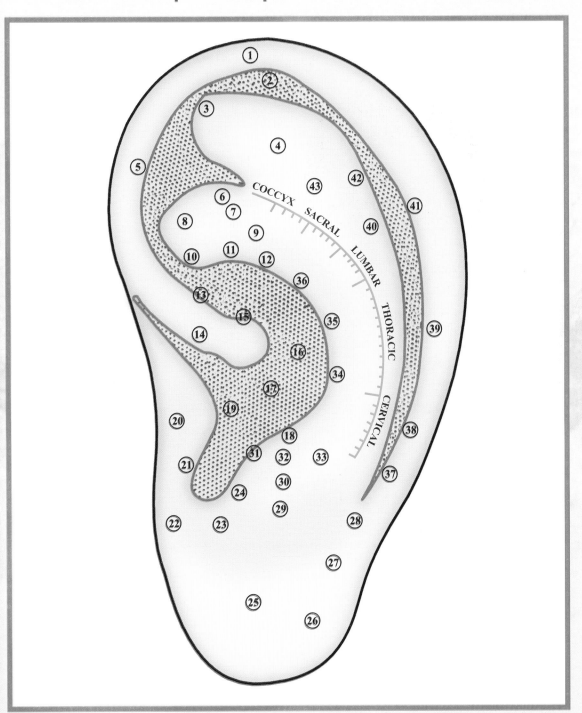

Treatment details related to the points on ears

1. Tonsil
2. Apendix
3. Ankle
4. Knee Joint
5. High Blood Pressue
6. Asthma
7. Hips
8. Sciatica Nerve
9. Knees
10. Bladder
11. Right Vretix
12. Kidney
13. Large Intestine
14. Rectum
15. Small Instentine
16. Stomach
17. Respiratory System
18. Lungs
19. Lungs
20. High Blood Pressure
21. Internal portion of Nose
22. Eyes
23. Eyes
24. Ovary
25. Eyes
26. Internal portion of Ear
27. Upper Jaw
28. Lower Jaw
29. Lungs
30. Testes
31. Asthma
32. Brain
33. Toothache
34. Liver
35. Spleen
36. Pancreas, Gall Bladder
37. Neck
38. Shoulder Bone
39. Shoulder
40. Stomach
41. Elbow
42. Knee
43. Hip Joint

Yog Sadhna
&
Yoga Healing Secrets

A person can do self-medication in this way through acupressure

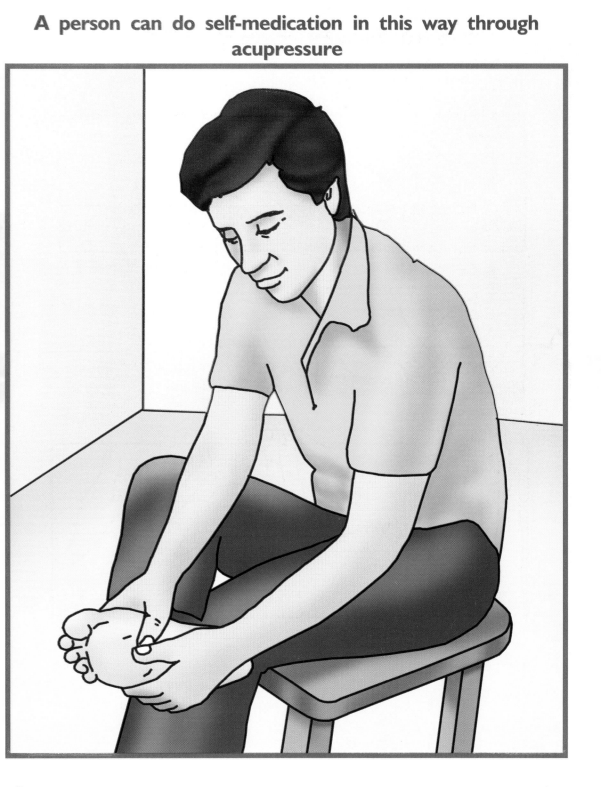

Different methods of giving acupressure

Correct method of applying pressure with big finger(thumb)

Wrong Method

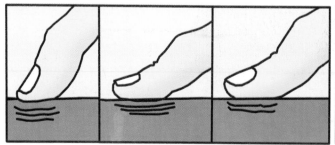

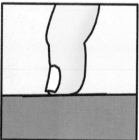

One should not lift the thumb while applying pressure

For applying more pressue one thumb should be kept on the other

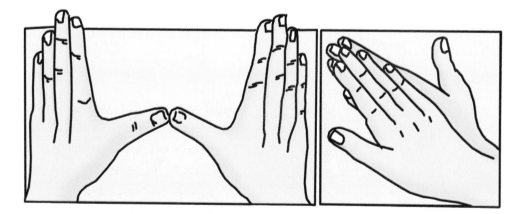

On some places, especially on the back apply pressure using both the thumbs.

One some centres, like stomach, apply pressue with these three fingers of both hands simultaneously.

Yog Sadhna
&
Yoga Healing Secrets

Life power centre situated on hand

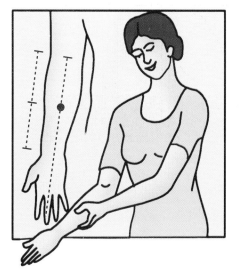

Pain relieving pressure points situated on the upper portion of hands and legs.

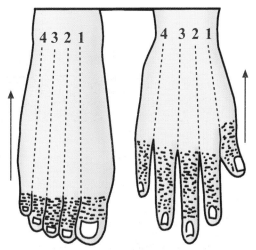

4 3 2 1   4 3 2 1

These points are same in both legs and hands.

A Illusive pains points

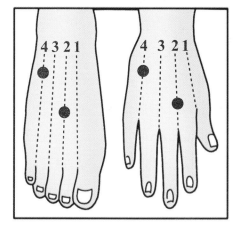

4 3 2 1   4 3 2 1

After using accupresure on thousands of patients for a long time, we have experienced that when pressure is applied on the four channels situated on the backside of hands and legs, the related pain is relaxed immediately. Apply pressure on these four points to relieve the pain of carrying spondalitis, frozen shoulder and pain at the back of the neck.

In the same way for pains related to sciatica, knees and other pains related to the legs, apply pressure on the pressure points of legs.

INTRODUCTION
Divya Yoga Mandir Trust, Kankhal

The headquarters of Divya Yoga Mandir Trust is located in Krupalu Bagh Ashram. Krupalu Bagh Ashram was established in 1932 by Shri Krupalu DevJiMaharaj, who belonged to warrior land, Mewad (Rajasthan) and his original name was Yeti Kishore Chand. During the independence revolution Kishorechandji played an active role in the freedom fight. He gave shelter to many revolutionists in Haridwar. Local freedom fighter Veni Prasad was one of the main partners. Yeti KishoreChand Ji established the first public library in Haridwar and with hard labor collected around 3500 books and kept them in the library located in the Upper Road. He established dozens of schools in this area to give a momentum to the task of building the nation. Founder of Gurukul Kangadi Swami ShradhanandJi had very good and close relations with him. Afterwards, Bal Gangadhar Tilak, Madan Mohan Malviya, Motilal Nehru, Mahatma Gandhi, Chittaranjan Das Munshi, Ganesh Sahankar Vidyarthi, V.J.Patel, Hakim Ajmal Khan came in close proximity.

Yeti Kishorechand associated with the Banga revolutionary party and took the responsibility of the bold task of circulating 'Yugantar" and "Lokantar" newspapers published by the party in northern India. The newspaper which was published in Bengali and English was pain in the neck of the Britishers. The foreign Government was afraid of this newspaper, which used was creating revolutionaries and exposing the Britishers. Yeti Kishorechand used to post these newspapers all over India in envelopes, sometimes from the Chandi Pahadi in Haridwar, sometimes from the library situated in Paliwala Dharmashala. During these days Banga revolutionary party assassinated Lord Harding in a bomb blast. Whose leader was Ras Behari Bose. Yeti Kishore ChandJi was given the responsibility to give shelter to Ras Behari Bose. At that time British

Government had kept a reward of Rs 3 lakhs on Ras Behari Bose. Yeti KishoreChand Ji gave him shelter in his ashram situated in the midst of forest. At that time his friend Harish Babu along with three other friends came to Haridwar and told that the Britishers have come to know the whereabouts of Ras Behari in Haridwar or Dehradun and they can raid the area at any time. Then Yeti Kishore Chand sent him to Varanasi in Dehradun Express in the disguise of Patiala tourist. Ras Behari boarded the night train to Varanasi and in the morning a huge army of policemen herded his hut. They searched every nook and corner for him but the lion was out of his cage and reached safely to Varanasi and from there he fled to Japan. The same Yeti KishoreChand became ascetic and came to be known as Krupalu Maharaj. He published a monthly magazine" Vishwa Gyan" to raise the flame of independence in the dependent India. Yeti Kishore Chand who was leading a life of freedom fighter and revolutionist was inspired towards Yoga and spirituality and he became an accomplished yogi. He left this world in 1968.

Disciples of Maharajji took over the responsibility of managing the pious , revolutionary, yoga devotion land Krupalu Bagh Asharm. Shri Swami Shankar Dev Ji is one of the bonds of this tradition, whose disciple Swami RamdevJi Maharaj has enlightened the ashram with the divine flame of yoga, Ayurveda, Vedic Culture and made it popular in the country, abroad, and the entire world. Divya Yoga mandir Trust which was established in 1995 and with this medium Swami Ramdev Ji Maharaj has with the help of his inseparable,   well-wishers namely Achrya KarmavirJi, Acharya BalkrishnaJi, Swami MuktanandJi, and others and with there co-operation has given shape to several services, projects, that has left deep impact on the Indian people and as a result Veda, Yoga, Ayurveda is flowing in the entire nation.

With the divine grace of these pious souls crores of people are getting the benefit of physical health, mental peace, self progress, spiritual development, and intelligence and are still getting it. He is equally moving ahead in the fields of Religion, Yoga, Spirituality, Social Service, Education, welfare of the mankind. Even then he has no ego, and he believes that we are only the medium and whatever is happening, or is going to happen is the result of God's desire and grace.

Services offered by Divya Yoga Mandir Trust

Various services have been started by the Divya Yoga Mandir Trust within a short period of one decade and the success story created through these services, is no less than a miracle for the people who are experiencing this. The multi dimensional form which the Paternal Yoga Pith is taking, the people are feeling that Swami Ramdevji is definitely blessed with some divine power. In fact all this is possible because of the pious feeling of respect, devotion towards God, determination of serving the people, welfare of the mankind. Swami in the mind of Ramdev baba and he is always inspired and active with these feelings. A summary of the various services offered by the Divya Yoga Mandir Trust is being given below:

Organization of yoga Practice and Yoga Healing Camps

Under the proximity of Revered Swami Ramdevji the yoga Devotion and Yoga Medication Camps organized all over the country have removed the myth that Yoga is only physical exercise. Revered SwamiJi has provided a definite meaningful and rational definition to Yoga by making it the basis for physical health, curing diseases, mental peace, self progress, intelligence and spiritual progress. The devotees who are regularly practicing Yoga are experiencing the benefits of Yoga. In these camps - education-training is given on eight principles of Yoga, resistance towards passions, rules, postures, pranayam, resisting sense, concentration,   meditation and deep meditation. Now the arrangements are being made for the study, regular study and training and utility based activity of Patanjali Yoga Sutra along with Hathyoga, Darshan, Upanishad,   Veda,

Charak, Sushrut and other texts. Arrangements are also being made to give practical training of Yoga, Shatkaram, Dhouti, Basti, Tratak, Nouli and Kapalbhati and along with these six yogic activities meditation Yoga and Devotion Yoga will also be included.

Brahmakalp Hospital

In Brahmakalp Hospital along with Shatkarma , Ayurvedic Panchkarma (Massage, fomentation, vomiting, evacuation of the bowels, basti), herbs and shrubs and essence -chemical based Ayurvedic Medicines, diet, digestion -indigestion, balanced celibacy and seasonal routine and daily routine are taught comprehensively and old and new diseases are cured. Acupressure, Yoga, and Asana, Pranayam, natural therapy training is being given free of cost and at very low costs for those who are unable to purchase these medicines due to insufficient funds.

Serious incurable diseases like high blood pressure, diabetes, heart problem, asthma, obesity, acidity, allergy, ulcer, cervical spondalitis, sciatica, arthritis, cancer (first and second stage) and others are cured without operation.

In the process of giving an extensive form to Brahma Kalp Hospital in Patanjali Yogapith, a residential hospital is also being created so that the patient can get admitted for treatment.

Respected Swami Ramdevji Maharaj says that we should all try that no disease should attack us.

Even if it happens we should first adopt Yoga and try to improve with it. Even if we have to take medicine we should give priority to Ayurvedic medicines because they are associated with our land, culture and nature and totally harmless. For this purpose it is necessary to have the medicines manufactured in specialized manner at Divya

Pharmacy containing quality medicines therefore in order to facilitate cheap and qualitative medicines Divya Yoga Mandir Trust has established Divya Pharmacy in the ashram premises, where medicines are manufactured in pure, qualitative manner, according to the classical principles using Self experience of Yoga, ash, mud, gold, essence, chemical, guggul, powder, globule, extractions, decoctions, ghee, oil, iron etc. We are fully trying to see that the medicnes manufactured should be pure, according to the classics and of high quality. Along with this we are providing these medicines at very low prices to the mankind so that they can avail these medicines easily. We are able to manufacture the medicines in limited quantity only, many times the people are disappointed due to non-availability of the medicines.

Therefore, a plan is being finalized to expand the Divya Pharmacy as early as possible, so that your requirements and your feeling towards us, can be fulfilled.

Laboratory

Divya Yoga Mandir Trust has its own laboratory whose works includes discovery of new medicines, finding the medicines which are not available for very long time, testing the quality of herbs purchased for Divya Pharmacy, determine the manufacture of medicines according to classical texts, to obtain the information about the medication and pharmacy fields, learn about new technique developed and researcher carried on this field, purchase books written on Ayurveda for the library, preservation and protection of medicinal plants, thinking about the commercial benefits and prepare literature and get it published. Other than practicing the traditional medicines.

The laboratory has developed several self applied yoga and has established a mile stone in the whole world. Since hundreds of years, non-availability of four medicinal plants of Ashtavarga was considered that these natural plants have lost their existence due to natural reasons. But due to the hard labor, deep interest and focused devotion of the laboratory technicians, these four plants could be found in the snow cladded mountains of Himalayas. A book by trust written on Ashtvarga mentions this discovery in detail.

Divya Medicinal Garden

A practical effort is being made in the ashram premises to preserve, conserve and increase the life-giving herbs, which are difficult to obtain and procure and available in the Himalayan region and other nations However due to lack of space, this project could not be given the desired form. Now ample space is available in Patanjali Yoga Pith for this purpose and plans are being made to grow the plants on a large scale and preserve them. The fresh essence of the plants and leaves and roots necessary for the medication will be taken care of in the Divya Medicinal Garden in the near future. The plants and seeds planted in the pots will be made available for sale.

Establishing Divya Byre (Goshala)

The mission for the preservation, improvisation and manufacture of medicines requires cow milk, cow urine, dung, and the mission to preserve the Indian breed of cattle for the service of cow and protect its breed, is going since long time in the ashram. Now in Patanjali Yoga Pith this is being given a broader look, in which thousands of cows will be taken care of. The dung obtained from this will be used as compost manure or bio-technical manure so that the food grains, fruits, vegetables, milk can be available which would be free of chemical fertilizers. Biogas will be manufactured from dung with which the daily needs of ashram will be fulfilled. The domestic breed of these cattle will be used to increase the cattle breed so that the cows cane be respected and protected.

Vedic Ritual

Agnihotra is a science in itself. Rituals have a special place in the Indian tradition in purifying the environment, balancing the atmosphere, making the seasons favorable, increasing the plants an their preservation, controlling the situation in case of drought and floods, to cure some diseases, and to accomplish the religious rituals. Following this saintly tradition, rituals are performed in the ashram everyday. There is a proposal to construct a huge yagnashala (ritual room) in the premises of Patanjali Yoga Pith. Scientific research and study will be conducted on the useful points of sacrifice or ritual.

Vedic Gurukul

A vedic Gurukul is being managed in Kishangarh-Ghaseda, 8 km from Rewadi in Haryana to maintain the vedic tradition, culture, high ideals, modern education fields, which provides education free of cost, in which the poor and rural children are gaining good culture and good education along with the children of higher society. There is still requirement of constructing a building so that maximum number of people can obtain education.

Devotion Ashram situated at Gangotri

Divya Yoga Mandir Trust has established an ashram in Gangotri for the devotees and to procure the rare herbs for the preservation and research of medicinal plants which are found in the Himalayan region, which needs to be given a wider form.

Establishment of Patanjali Yoga Pith

Patanjali Yoga Pith is a multi- dimensional project of the original institution Divya Yog Mandir Trust, which will occupy an area of one lakh thousand hectares. It will play a major role in the communication, training, research of Veda, Yoga, Ayurveda. This will provide hostel facility to around two thousand devotees. It will be a building containing 1500 rooms, and will be equipped with pharmacy, hospital, cattle ground, herbs nursery, yoga Sandesh and Literature publishing and sales research department, library, printing press, kitchen, Yoga center, ritual room, and other facilities. The people coming into the premises will get pure and pious food, which will be separate from L.P.G. chemcial fertilizers, and pesticides. This premises will be developed like Rabindranath Tagore's Shantiniketan and will be fully self-reliant which will provide health. yoga practice, mental peace, and spiritual development to crores of people. This will take the shape of revered devotional field in the whole world. Swami Ji has taken the vow to complete the multi- dimensional project worth Rs 100 crores with the co-operation of crores of devotees, which is being fulfilled with the blessings of Supreme Soul.

The fund amount fixed by the trust for the purpose of membership of Yoga pith is as follows:

1.	Founder member	Rs 5,00,000
2.	Patron member	Rs 2, 51,000
3.	Life Member	Rs 1,00,000
4.	Special Member	Rs 51,000
5.	Honoured Member	Rs 21,000
6.	Ordinary Member	Rs 11,000

Publishing of Yog Sandesh (Hindi, English, Marathi, Bengali, Punjabi and Gujrati monthly magazine)

Keeping in mind the demand of thousands of devotees associated with the Divya Yog Mandir Trust, 'Yog Sandesh" a monthly magazine is being published since September 2003 with the co-operation of experienced editorial team. The number of new readers being added every month is a proof of its increasing popularity. A resolution has been taken to spread Yoga, Ayurveda, culture-tradition and spiritual thinking obtained from saintly tradition to lakhs of readers in the near future. Other than this, poems, useful articles for the people, activities of the trust, and future plans and readers experience will also be given place in the magazine. The extensive reach and circulation of a Hindi magazine within such a short time is the result of revered Swami Ramdev Ji Maharaj's profound influence.